The Secular Relevance of the Church

CHRISTIAN PERSPECTIVES
ON SOCIAL PROBLEMS

Gayraud S. Wilmore, *General Editor*

The Secular Relevance of the Church

by
GAYRAUD S. WILMORE

BOARD OF CHRISTIAN EDUCATION
The United Presbyterian Church U.S.A.
Witherspoon Building
Philadelphia, Pa. 19107

COPYRIGHT © MCMLXII W. L. JENKINS

All rights reserved—no part of this book may be reproduced in any form without permission in writing from the publisher, except by a reviewer who wishes to quote brief passages in connection with a review in magazine or newspaper.

Scripture quotations from the Revised Standard Version of the Bible are copyright, 1946 and 1952, by the Division of Christian Education of the National Council of Churches, and are used by permission.

LIBRARY OF CONGRESS CATALOG CARD No. 62–14177

PRINTED IN THE UNITED STATES OF AMERICA

Contents

Foreword	1
I. The Protestant Trap	3
II. Spurious Secularism and True Secularity	17
III. The Faithful Use of Power	37
IV. The Equipment of the Saints	61
Questions for Study and Discussion	87

Foreword

THIS BOOK IS A SPECIAL EDITION OF THE FIRST volume of the new series Christian Perspectives on Social Problems. It has been chosen as the first annual study book for United Presbyterian church officers. It is our hope that throughout the year elders, deacons, and trustees will be reading, studying, and discussing together the problems and issues raised in this book.

Why an annual study book for church officers? In our presbyterian system of representative government the elected officers, mainly the session, are largely responsible for leading and directing the work of the congregation. They make the decisions and lay the plans that determine the policy and program of the local church. A church officer cannot adequately discharge this responsibility unless he is striving to understand why the church exists and what God is calling the church to do in a particular community. In short, he must grapple with theological issues. Leading an exemplary personal life and performing routine committee chores is *not* enough.

So, we must say to the church officer who thinks in terms of the "practical" work of the church that theological understanding and "practical" church business belong together. Church policies and programs expressed in the organizational work of the congregation should serve the missionary purpose for which the church exists. In this sense, continuing theological study is not an elective for those officers who happen to be interested in such matters but is as integral a part of the work of the church officer as attending meetings and undertaking committee assignments. The ministry of a local church to its community will be more faithful and relevant as its officers bring to bear upon their practical decisions a deepened awareness of what God is seeking to do through his church.

THE SECULAR RELEVANCE OF THE CHURCH has been selected because it explores, in a practical and realistic way, one of the central issues facing Protestantism, Can the church make a relevant and redemptive witness in the secular society of today? No one can deny that the increasing secularization of our culture, together with the growth of a religiously pluralistic society, has diminished the influence of the Protestant Church in our national life. The author spotlights particular areas of weakness in our traditional Protestant approach to secular culture and offers concrete suggestions as to how a local congregation can provide a more effective ministry to its community. A careful study of this book will be of immense practical value to church officers. Questions for discussion are included at the end of the book.

CORNELIUS O. BERRY

SUGGESTED COLLATERAL READING

Beyond Religion, by Daniel Jenkins. The Westminster Press. $2.75.

The New Creation as Metropolis, by Gibson Winter. The Macmillan Company. $3.95.

The Noise of Solemn Assemblies, by Peter L. Berger. Doubleday & Company, Inc. Paperback, $1.75.

The Protestant and Politics, by William Lee Miller. The Westminster Press. $1.00.

Chapter I

The Protestant Trap

> When . . . [Protestantism] ceases to express the work of God in its cultural dimension, it just disappears. . . . There is a beautiful "Indian Summer"; everything seems to stand still. It is extremely difficult to decide whether you are in life or in death, whether it is autumn or spring. . . . I may be wrong, but just now the sweetness of autumnal decay seems to be upon it.—Coert Rylaarsdam, *The Doctrine of the Church and the Problem of Culture.*

This book begins with a question at the heart of the present ecumenical interest in the nature and mission of the church of Christ in the modern world. It is not a new question. It is an old one, but we can no longer avoid dealing with it in a most radical and challenging form. It may be stated in this way: Can the church of Christ, as represented in this discussion by the Protestant churches, become an effective influence for basic change and reconstruction in a highly technological, secularized society?

Behind this question is an assumption that will serve usefully to sharpen the focus of the debate to follow in these pages. It is the assumption that for all the scattered evidence of Protestant interest in "being involved" in the solution of social problems, Protestant churches continue to understand the nature and mission of the church in terms of preaching Sunday sermons, saving souls, and inculcating the moral standards of a traditionalistic and rural society. There is among most Protestant churches, consequently, a studied avoidance of the role of organizing institutional power and a commitment to social action as a basic strategy of mission.

The question that we must immediately face, therefore, is whether such a church can ever hope to have any considerable influence in the struggle for freedom and justice in a revolutionary world. It should be noted that we are here concerned mainly about conditions in American society and the relation of the Protestant churches to the American scene. But what we have to consider obviously relates to the church of Christ everywhere. It is perhaps even more urgent in Africa and Asia, where rapid industrialization is in process and will have to be established upon cultural foundations almost entirely lacking of the Judaeo-Christian elements that are present in European and American societies. Will the younger churches, with their similar fixation upon personal spirituality and morality, be relevant to the crucial human problems of these new nations?

The argument we will present does not have to do with whether or not individual persons are of ultimate concern to God and should be the object of the mission of the church. That question has already been answered. The Bible and almost two thousand years of church history and theology have answered it affirmatively. We have no sound reason for discarding that answer even though, in attempting to discover what it means today, we may seem to be denying its validity. Nor are we considering here, by the manner in which we have stated our basic question and the rather bold assumption that underlies it, whether or not the church of Christ can dominate secular society, whether it can today undertake political action as a full-blown political party, or erect a new

"Christian economic system" to replace present systems. These are already dubious possibilities for the church, even in Europe and Latin America, where such traditions have had an uneasy but accepted place in the culture.

OLD THEOLOGY IN A NEW AGE

Our question is, rather, whether a religion that speaks only about love, humility, sobriety, personal integrity, honesty, and other individualistic virtues has any real possibility of changing the world in which we live. We are asking whether these otherwise honorable virtues have any possibility of relevant meaning or of realization in a rationalized, technological society unless the churches recover a comprehensive cultural vocation that has a great deal more to say than this, and is able to speak through social and political action.

Paul Abrecht, in *The Churches and Rapid Social Change,* lists three reasons why the old theology of the church cannot meet the challenge of social change in the new nations of the world. He might well have used the same arguments for the American situation. First of all, says Abrecht, the old theological ethical formulations do not provide the theological basis for an ethical analysis and criticism of social problems. Secondly, they do not help people to evaluate customary forms of community life and values. Thirdly, the old formulations do not provide an adequate "theological-ethical basis for relating the scientific study of social institutions to the development of Christian social policy."

The traditional themes of the old theology—personal salvation and individualistic morality—do not occupy the place in American Protestant theology today that they once did, but to think that they have been banished from the ethos of Protestant Church life is to be deluded. In fact, these two themes have never really been absent from American Protestantism at any time. They have served, in every generation, to prevent the church from coming to grips with the deepest issues of social justice. Men like Lyman Abbott, George Herron, and Walter Rauschenbusch sought to make the church rise to the problems of industrial society when those problems were first emerging. Their concerns were not superficial. They compared, for example, the classical theory of economics with the new socialism of their day, the conflicting interests of capital and labor, the new metropolitanism with the rural ways of life. None of these issues, however, had been entirely absent from the earlier reforming zeal that grew out of the revivalistic preaching which followed the Second Great Awakening. Nor did the social gospelers disengage them from theological conservatism.

Before 1850, the preaching of Charles G. Finney and other revivalists, linked individual salvation, free will, and moralism to the question of how the Christian should fight social evil. That connection has continued, almost undisturbed, to the present. Because of its basic orientation to the belief that great social problems are solved by converting individuals, it has successfully blunted the edge of any realistic analysis of social problems and any effective strategy of church action. There may be a few exceptions, but they are few indeed.

The social gospel, for all its pragmatism, was never quite free of "ethical revivalism," which really had to do with saving souls. This pious reformism always threatened to frustrate a realistic approach to social action. A study of the early pronouncements of the Federal Council of Churches, formed in 1908 as a social gospel stronghold, will show that it is difficult to tell where revivalistic social concern breaks off and the "mature" social gospel begins. Rauschenbusch himself believed that the revivalistic orthodoxy, with its emphasis on the simplicity of reli-

THE PROTESTANT TRAP

gion and its solution to all the problems of life, was not wholly incompatible with his own views.

"I have entire sympathy," he wrote, "with the conservative instinct which shrinks from giving up any of the dear possessions which have made life holy for us. We have none too much of them left. It is a comfort to me to know that the changes required to make room for the social gospel are not destructive but constructive."

It is questionable, however, whether those changes were ever brought about and whether room was actually made for a Protestantism that could attack the problems of society with effect. Liberal Protestantism and the social gospel brought an enlarged vision to the American churches, but its close connection with the mixture of conservatism and Pelagianism of the revivalists prevented its deepest implications from ever really becoming an alternative to what was already assumed to be "social Christianity" by the American church public.

A few ministers and seminary professors understood the new direction the social gospel movement indicated at its best. Some of them could not remain in the church and found their way into the Socialist Party, the trade-union movement, and other social action groups. These men saw that the social gospel, for all its theological deficiencies which, of course, did not concern them, demanded a radical new social and political ethos for the church. But the turn in the road from orthodoxy, which had been engineered by Rauschenbusch and others, had not been sharp enough to lead in a new direction. It could not bring an authentic reconstruction of the social order, nor a new relationship between the church and American culture.

Those who left the organized church appear now to have been reasonably correct in their assumption. A nonpolitical, social welfare Protestantism, devoid of any scientific social analysis or much interest in social action, has persisted in the churches until today. Indeed, as the suburban, middle-class mentality, with its commitment to peace, piety, and prosperity, becomes almost standard for most churchmen in the United States, this kind of Protestantism may well have increased. The work of the church-sponsored Anti-Saloon League during the campaign for national prohibition from 1912 to 1918 sounds impressively realistic and effective today, but the issue was then liquor—since the colonial period a favorite whipping boy for American Protestants. Action on many other less obvious issues, upon which church pronouncements are made, has continued to be individualistic, oriented to "attitudinal-change," sentimental, and crusading.

Intelligence in political analysis, the sense of a relationship between what C. Wright Mills has called "troubles" and "issues," sensitivity to the realities of power, acceptance of controversy as normative for democratic action, and recognition of the necessity of corporate action —all these, and other elements introduced by the early writings of Reinhold Niebuhr and other social ethicists, are missing in most American Protestant churches today. It is as if the best of the social gospel movement and the ethical realism of neo-orthodoxy had never happened. Instead of these correctives to theological conservatism we hear emphases and points of view intimately connected to the themes of revivalism from Finney to Graham— moralism and piecemeal reform in temperance, gambling, Sabbath observance, and relations with the Vatican. Ministers and laymen seem hesitant to speak frankly of such basic realities as class stratification, racial discrimination, the fact of power politics and economic determinism. We hear also the refusal to acknowledge that changes in social structure which remove certain barriers to justice and brotherhood may have to precede individual conversions. This is the general tenor of Protestant discussion about social problems, especially at the local church level, if such problems are discussed at all. Some progress toward relevant social analysis and action has undoubtedly been made, but it is difficult to see that most of American Protestantism has moved very far from the ethical revivalism of the last century.

All of this is not to say that the theological-ethical themes of personal salvation and individual morality have not borne some fruit for the social witness of the church in the history of modern Christianity. One has to respect the many examples of effective service to the underprivileged masses of the cities in Great Britain and the United States during the last quarter of the nineteenth century—such as the charitable work of Edward Denison in the London East End and the similar ministry of men like the Rev. Charles G. Ames of Germantown, Pennsylvania, as early as 1874. The "Darkest England" program of William Booth after 1890 and earlier Christian social service in industrial areas paved the way for the work that is being done today in Skid Row by the Salvation Army and the many downtown "rescue missions" headed by fundamentalist Bible institute graduates. This kind of social witness has its own unique significance and it often attracts interest and support from secularists who are more impressed by a soup line in the inner city than by the more sophisticated mission work of the main-line denominations among Indians and agricultural migrants. In some communities the social service and social action that stem from revivalism and its peculiar brand of conservatism is sensible and effective.

But one would have to admit that this is not usually the case. In one Eastern city, the pious appeal of the Lord's Day Alliance, according to some local politicians, did as much to make Protestants go out and vote for legalized gambling as it garnered votes against it. The Pentecostal and Holiness churches, which sometimes have more racial integration in their inner-city churches than the larger denominations, have attempted almost nothing in the field of public school integration, housing, and job opportunities for Negroes. Their racial integration can be impressive, but it is a Sunday affair and limited to born-again Christians. The Salvation Army does the work of the good Samaritan in the urban areas while the other denominations ride by on the new expressways in their station wagons. But soup, crackers, and a dormitory bed if you will listen to an evangelistic sermon is no substitute for social legislation and direct pressure on city authorities to do something about the problem of homeless men.

Even if we must admit that the personal salvation–individualistic morality approach has been effective in the past, it would not work in the future. The Protestant ethical currency, which could formerly depend upon a fairly general "Christian conscience" in the culture, is being increasingly devalued. It cannot be turned in for the public sense of sinfulness and willingness to repent that it once commanded among urbanites in this country. With the growing religious pluralism and secularization of American society, there is little optimism for the public influence of the Protestant Church when it depends upon an appeal to traditional morality and the gospel of individual salvation.

The times are changing. There is today an ever-widening chasm between the mountaintop experiences of eleven o'clock Sunday morning and the rest of the hours of the week in the workaday world. The hymns and prayers wafting from the half-empty inner-city churches are all but drowned out by the noise of the "exploding metropolis" and the thunder of the industrial machine. God still seeks and finds men and women in the city despite the many barriers technological progress has thrown up before him. But the preaching on an individualistic gospel, the peace-of-heart-and-mind pabulum, the exhortations to love our depersonalized neighbors and live with quiet assurance about the radioactive future and a "heaven" whose traditional geography has been penetrated by rockets and astronauts are all being crudely heckled by the hard realities of the world in which we live.

Given the main theological emphases of American Protestantism from the beginning of modern revivalism at the Great Cane Ridge camp meeting of 1801 to Oral Roberts and the failure of the social gospel ever to affect deeply the churchgoing public, no one should be surprised at this turn of affairs.

The Church in a Changing Society

In the middle of the nineteenth century this country began to move rapidly from a predominately rural to a predominately urban civilization. The great new inventions that culminated in the mass production industries of today required a concentration of capital and labor and the reorganization of both to fit the needs of a new era of industrial expansion. The cities grew down the new highways that were built to accommodate an increasingly mobile populace. Between the First and the Second World Wars the Gross National Product rose from 77.5 to 125.3 billions of dollars; the national income went from 68 billions in 1919 to 104 billions in 1941. But in 1940 the national income was produced with four million fewer workers than were employed at the beginning of the depression. Machines were replacing workers rapidly while the population was rising—from slightly more than one hundred million during the First World War to one hundred and thirty-three million at the beginning of the Second.

With the tremendous growth and expansion of business and government during and after World War II, the great shift of power from the individual and the small

12 SECULAR RELEVANCE OF THE CHURCH

groups of society to great collectivities became more and more evident. A steady, tarantulalike encroachment was being made by business, industry, and government upon the functions of the family, the school, the neighborhood church, and the other primary institutions of the American community.

It is no wonder that peace of heart and mind are difficult to conceive and more difficult to justify where everyone is "getting and spending" to keep up with the mad race for material possessions now available in unprecedented abundance. Activity oriented to personal consumption, achievement and rapid upward mobility, with increased nostalgia but decreased utilization of the old ways and old things, are evidently hallmarks of a competitive, profit-hungry economy. It becomes highly dubious what "loving one's neighbor" means when most of one's decisions are made by someone else and impersonality is a protective device against strangers with whom one competes for transportation, discount bargains, jobs, and residences. And it becomes more and more difficult to live with quiet assurance about the future under the shadow of the bomb.

Nor has the phenomenal growth of the institutional church from 16 per cent of the population in 1850 to 63 per cent in 1960, and the leap in valuation of religious buildings constructed from one hundred and sixty-five million dollars in 1925 to a billion, sixteen million dollars today, succeeded, with all the evidences of the health of the religious enterprise, in blinding us to the fact that we are in a Protestant "Indian Summer." The popularity of religion among the middle classes after the Second World War, and the successes of Sheen, Peale, Graham, and Mahalia Jackson's gospel songs have not made us insensitive to the pervasive aroma of decay. As Martin Marty points out in his *The New Shape of American Religion,* after each new revival of interest in religion, the American people have suffered, with seeming inevitability, a more dismal aftermath than the last.

If, as opposed to Roman Catholicism, it is the vocation of Protestantism to transform secularism without an ecclesiastical domination of the culture, we have yet to demonstrate that transformation is taking place. What we view today is not the expression of authentic Protestantism in its cultural vocation. When we have the courage to be honest about it we must grant that it looks much more like a quiet, genteel Protestantism in cultural decay.

In the case of the individual congregation and its immediate neighborhood situation the picture may be more complex but less confusing. We know very well that we have lost much that is authentic in Christianity in the last few years. We have talked a great deal and with embarrassment about the necessity of the church being "in the world." Here at the local level in terms of prestige, the respectful bows of the political and business communities, and the daily activities of ministers and laymen—the church is very much *in* the world. There has obviously been little profound thinking about *how* the church should be in the world as we know it today and whether the world should be permitted to make the decision about *where* we should be in it.

Today the church is in the world—but much as a parenthesis is in a sentence and could quite easily be deleted without great effect. The church has a place assigned to it as a marginal form of social organization characterized by informal status group activities, which are reserved for Sundays or for occasional gatherings during the week. It does, as the sociologists say, integrate certain values and gives sanction to certain norms that other institutions originate for the really important concerns of Monday through Saturday. But it is not integral with the culture—certainly not in the way that government and business are integral. Most of the congregations we know are class churches that reflect only the sentimentalized, "spiritual" aspects of community life. They are segmental. They mind their own spiritual business by quietly filling their assigned places in the table of community organizations along with the home, the school, the supermarket, and the courthouse. Like the church of a certain manorial village in the thirteenth century, they stand, figuratively if not physically, outside of the village proper, away from the busy crosscurrents of village life, but near the manor house where the lord or his representative lives.

One may say that such a church is in the world; for people continue to come and go, and it has its assigned tasks to perform. The world, although it would soon recover, would be shocked and offended if the church should one day say: "We haven't anything to do with you. Don't send us your scrubbed children, nor your happy families any more. Don't ask us for contributions to your Community Chest and invocations for your public meetings and banquets. Don't honor us any longer with your tax exemptions and your department-store discounts. This relationship has been a horrible mistake. We have something quite different to do with you and say to you than you have supposed."

But the churches, for the most part, have no intention of making such a declaration of independence from this comfortable relationship. They continue to believe that they exist in a Protestant Christian nation and that American culture is still permeable to the message of individual salvation, peace of mind, and the virtues of the Sermon on the Mount. And they also believe that—with the possible exception of the communist world—all of this is quite compatible with the modern spirit and especially with the aspirations of the American nation to which God has unquestionably given the mantle of world leadership.

And so laymen, momentarily suppressing mental images

of the things that happen to them during the week, sit in the Sunday pews and muse over the slim possibility that the presence of the American flag beside the pulpit symbolizes a Christian—a Protestant Christian—nation where the Ten Commandments and the teachings of Jesus provide immediate answers to economic, political, social, and personal problems if only we would use them. Ministers, without more than a grudging acknowledgment of the forces that have invaded the home and torn the family asunder, continue to tell their congregations that "the family that prays together stays together." Church social action committees still deal with community problems with the assumption that if only the attitudes and hearts of their neighbors could be changed, their neighbors' practices would automatically conform to the ideals of justice and brotherhood.

What is the inevitable result of this kind of fuzzy, wishful thinking about the relationship between the church and culture? It is nothing less than a kind of religious play-acting—a dogged but weary chipping away at the rock of secularism with the faint hope that it will yet spring open and emit streams of living water.

But are we not on a treadmill of deception? Millions of dollars are raised to build beautiful new educational wings for our churches only to see the children, who rarely use them after junor high school age, captured by a culture which insists that the mind is a tool by which one jimmies the lock on happiness and material security. Sermons on moral autonomy and integrity are preached Sunday after Sunday to lower-eschelon business personnel whose every decision is made in a framework of bureaucratic authority that enforces its own understanding of virtue by a rigid discipline. We try to make twenty-minute filmstrips and "Dial-a-Prayer" compete with the gargantuan mass media and all the daily pressures that communicate the message that the whole world is nothing but a big pie for everyone to dig in and slice as best he can. We work for years to build great urban churches only to see our parishes disintegrate in panic when the Southern mountaineers, Negroes, and Puerto Ricans move into the neighborhoods that were thought to be so dedicated to democracy and brotherhood.

And so we Protestant churchmen work hard, but we are on a treadmill. We are sincere, sacrificing, generous with time and money, loyal to our weary and harassed pastors, attentive to sermons, church bulletins, and denominational literature, but, sadly enough, without really understanding what is going on—what is happening to the church or to ourselves. We are, in fact, caught in a cultural trap which, in terms of its tyranny over our essential humanity, its defection from the deepest sources of the Judaeo-Christian heritage, its almost irresistable determination of our thoughts and actions, has all the characteristics of that which the New Testament knows as the demonic. There is nothing left for us but to fight our way out.

Chapter II

Spurious Secularism and True Secularity

Secularism is a protest against . . . sacrifice of the fullness of life in the name of a man-made unity. Of course, secularism itself is in danger of setting up an ideological system as idolatrous as any other religious system or degenerating into lawlessness and thus betraying its own protest. But there is a deep Christian truth in the secular protest, namely, that the different spheres of human life have a real autonomy and must not be regimented into a narrow unity easily achieved through the religious integration of society.—M. M. Thomas, *Christian Participation in Nation-Building.*

We have spoken critically, sometimes harshly, of the old theological-ethical emphasis upon a gospel of personal salvation and an individualistic morality better suited for a rural culture than for the megalopolis of today. Does this mean a repudiation of the person-centered elements in the New Testament and in Christian faith and life? Our answer is that we must find theological formulations which are most relevant today, which are no less Biblical, and which develop these themes in a new context. Far from dropping out of the Christian faith a concern for the individual, we must locate the individual and minister to his needs in his real situation before God and his brother.

The question before the churches today is not whether they should disavow the personal meaning of faith—the fact that God calls each of us by name and empowers us to live in a way that transcends the pain, frustration, and tragedy of existence. The question is how the churches can understand the meaning of this personal dimension of faith within a larger context. It is not the work of Christ for individuals that must bear the full meaning and significance of God's cosmic work. It is, rather, God's cosmic work, the redemption of total reality, that must be understood to bear the full meaning and significance of what he has done and is doing for individuals.

There are indeed moments when the church has nothing to do for a man except to hold his hand and commend his soul to God. Every Christian who has been a priest to another person knows that such moments come. When love is in desperation to know what to do, sometimes God acts miraculously to bring courage and hope and new life where all our ministrations fail. There is a peace that passes understanding and a spiritual strength, not of man nor of worldly panaceas, which God can give to a man when he has been stripped of all defenses and lies broken and naked in the gutter of life. But the church has no business to define its ministry in these terms, as if its normative response to human extremity is to pray for some miraculous occurrence in the inwardness of the soul quite apart from human help. When this does happen, it is because God has taken the matter out of our hands and not because he has nothing for us to do except "preach the gospel, say our prayers, and let the chips fall where they may." If the miracle of grace happens, it is because Christ is the Lord of the universe and God has placed all power on earth and in heaven under his feet—not because God has limited his activity to the practice of divine surgery upon the souls of men.

What we can say about a God whose divine presence is in the solitude and inwardness of individuals cannot be separated from our knowledge of his action in the structures of society and the politics of nations. Indeed, we can say that history is the context in which he has to do with us as individuals because we look at history from the point of view of faith in the Lordship of Christ. History from this point of view has cosmic dimensions. It concerns the here and now, the concrete and time-bound. At the same time, it overarches all time and space and has its beginning and end, its purpose and meaning, in a reality that is beyond itself.

This is what it means to speak of the God and Father of Jesus Christ as the God of men and nations. The man of faith knows of His presence at both levels of experience and he also knows that they so impinge upon and interpenetrate each other as to become one. This is why he cannot speak of the inwardness of faith without speaking at the same time of its outwardness. He cannot separate the sacred and the secular, the authority of structures in human life from the authority of spirit, the works of love from the works of justice. He cannot, in any ultimate sense, disengage the salvation of individuals from the creation of the world and cosmic redemption through Jesus Christ.

It is perhaps more comforting to maintain these dualities of nineteenth-century orthodoxy. It is like being able always to go home to mother if the marriage does not work out. But the man of faith is not bound to the comfortable security of this kind of dualistic thinking. He is bold enough to believe that he lives in one world, knows of one reality, and worships one God who, in Jesus Christ, has once for all torn down the barriers between heaven and earth.

The New Secularity: "Holy Worldliness"

This is why the church today is beginning to hear voices—especially from the younger churches—calling it to a holy worldliness or secularity as a new basis for its missionary activity. The church has been "worldly" before, but theologians like Emil Brunner and Hans Ruedi Weber speak of "holy worldliness' in quite a different sense from aping the conventions and values of unregenerate men. The worldliness of the church, as we have seen, was an assignment from the culture and not from the Creator-Judge-Redeemer of the world. We can say that it was a phony worldliness that sought to make the churches uncritically acceptable to the culture on its own terms.

The American churches of the late '40's and '50's, at least in the main-line denominations, saw themselves in the image of a community Y.M.C.A., but with something less than the common sense of a good Y.M.C.A. about its own limitations and its obligation to serve anyone who wanted to use its facilities. The worldliness of the churches was expressed by taking the traditional prohibitions off dancing, smoking, playing cards, showing motion pictures in the sanctuary—and somewhat more gingerly, social drinking. The minister of the middle-class church was now "one of the boys," and the monthly program meetings, the gibes and wisecracks, the cigars and cigarettes in the men's fellowship, made it practically indistinguishable from the Rotary Club or Kiwanis.

But the churches never attained to a true and profound secularity that understood what worldliness was about and how God chooses to consecrate it among the saints for his redemptive purposes. The churches were not made up of secular men and women who had heard the gospel and were opening new frontiers in the world for its proclamation and demonstration. They were composed of "religious people" who were, in the upwardly mobile middle-class churches, basically oriented to political and theological conservatism. These good people, in the climate created by the social disorganization and recovery of the

Roosevelt years, learned that it was possible to be slightly daring about behavior and still be acceptable in Christian circles. This new freedom had almost nothing to do with their understanding of the gospel or of the nature and mission of the church.

Wherein lies the true secularity of the church? It is in believing and acting out realistically the message that Jesus Christ is not only the Lord of the church but is also the Lord of General Motors and the Democratic Party and is working quite outside the church as such, to fulfill the reconciliation of the world. There is, with respect to the church as church, a chosen secularity, a holy worldliness that aids and abets an authentic secularism, with respect to the world as world. This authentic secularism is a humanistic idealism based upon reason and a universalistic ethic that, in our own time, has been chastened by some of the imponderable realities of man's condition in the world. Although it does not acknowledge Jesus Christ as Lord, it has nevertheless absorbed into its concern for freedom and justice some of the revolutionary spirit of his life and teaching. It is his unwitting instrument for the humanization of technological society, for the renovation of truth and beauty, for the defense of political freedom and social justice. Alongside of it, the church, whenever it responds to God's call to a holy secularity in its own life, fights against the spurious secularism which is nothing more than America's soul-saving, moralistic "religion-in-general."

We are not to suppose that this authentic secularism of some of our unchurched contemporaries is not under judgment. As M. M. Thomas has said, it can be "as idolatrous as any other religious system" and can break out into a demonic lawlessness. It has its share of *hubris,* or human pride. But it is very often a reaction against the pride and vainglory of the church. It is under judgment, as Babylonia was under judgment during Israel's captivity; but like Babylonia, it is also the bearer of God's judgment against his recalcitrant and faithless people.

It may well be that Protestantism in its decay has nothing left that is distinctively relevant to secularism except the faith, deeply submerged in the Reformation heritage, that God is working outside the church as well as within it. The challenge to American Protestants today is to have enough faith in the sovereignty and wisdom of God to believe that there is extant in the world an authentic secularism which is not only legitimate in its own right but has a peculiar form and purpose in the missionary church.

There is a brand of Christian fundamentalism that comes both in Roman Catholic and Protestant varieties which refuses to grant a legitimate role to secularism in the divine purpose. Although this is somewhat ambiguous in both brands of fundamentalism in the history of the church, one can say that for them the reconciliation of the world to God generally requires one of two positions. The secular must give up its autonomy and become obedient to the law of nature as it is perceived and interpreted by the church, or individuals must disentangle themselves from the trappings of the secular as such in order to return to it as citizens who, within their own spheres of life, are now able to practice the superior morality of "Christian politics" or "Christian economics."

The 1954 Report of the Lay Committee of the National Council of Churches, which was disbanded by the National Council in 1955 over a controversy about social pronouncements, read in part: "Our committee believes that church organizations should devote their time and energy to saving souls and making Christians out of people; that once people have become Christians, they will evolve a government which can be depended upon to administer the affairs of state wisely and well."

This is a characteristic statement of one form of American religiosity which would be acceptable to many Protestants, and to many more Roman Catholics than the historic position of that church would lead one to suspect. Historically the views of the relation between the church and secularism in Roman Catholicism have tended to subsume all of culture—particularly, art, science, education, and politics—under natural law as interpreted by ecclesiastical authority. But in modern times the Roman Church has been flexible enough to modify this position to accord with existing circumstances. The American situation has certainly forced such modifications in official policy; and Catholic laymen, with or without pastoral approbation, have increasingly assimilated the point of view represented by the Report of the Lay Committee.

But in either case we are dealing essentially with the rejection of the secular as such. This view believes that there is something fundamentally wrong with worldliness. The church either must subject it to the Christian way of life, or must break with the world and help Christians to create within it enclaves of holiness. This latter situation does not mean, however, that a man is not able to continue a reasonably high margin of profit in his business and use economic and political power to resist undesirable elements in his neighborhood and creeping socialism in Washington.

Protestantism has oscillated at times between the two poles of cultural domination and cultural retreat. In its exclusivistic sectarian form it has sought to create holy communities of good men who could be involved in worldly enterprises without worldly taint. In its universalistic denominational form it has sometimes sought to dominate the secular culture and, by means of moral crusades and pious influence in the right places, impose Christian standards upon it.

It has not been very long ago since one thousand Philadelphia clergymen decided what was an acceptable dress for women, and a reform committee of prominent citizens designed to their specifications a "moral gown," endorsed by the clergy of fifteen denominations. Frederick Lewis Allen writes concerning this "Christian garment" that it was "very loose-fitting, sleeves reached just below the elbows, and the hem came within seven and a half inches of the floor." A stifled yawn from the males in the pews is pardonable. There is probably nothing more jejune than a worldly enterprise that becomes captive to pietistic religion! Protestants, no less than Roman Catholics, have been tempted by the "religious umbrella" theory.

It is a mistake for the church to assume that every aspect of secular life must be moralized. Persons given to this attitude concerning worldly existence are constantly holding up the ethical imperatives of the church as an umbrella over the secular in every time, place, and situation. Concerning these ardent moralizers of life, Dietrich Bonhoeffer writes in his *Ethics:* "They seem to imagine that every human action has had a clearly lettered notice attached to it by some divine police authority, a notice which reads 'permitted' or 'forbidden.'. . . This represents a failure to understand that in historical human existence everything has its time (Eccl., ch. 3), eating, drinking, and sleeping as well as deliberate resolve and action, rest as well as work, purposelessness as well as the fulfillment of purpose, inclination as well as duty, play as well as earnest endeavor, joy as well as renunciation" (The Macmillan Company, 1955).

Protestantism, when it recognizes the most profound implications of the incarnation and of the Reformation doctrine of vocation, has nowhere to stand except with the secular. It refuses to make an idol of religion. It makes common cause with the authentically secular without being permanently wedded to it. It believes in the secular not only as an instrument of divine providence and judgment but also as a partner with the church in the work of reconciliation. For the faith of the church is that God has chosen worldly man in Jesus Christ, and with man, the civil order and the structures of secular society. Because Christ is Lord, the secular as such is within his domain. A Christological view of the secular, therefore, is one of the points at which a sociotheological perspective breaks with the older theological-ethical formulations of the relationship between the church and culture.

"For in him all things were created, in heaven and on earth, visible and invisible, whether thrones or dominions or principalities or authorities—all things were created through him and for him. He is before all things, and in him all things hold together." (Col. 1:16–17.)

The Lordship of Christ over the secular does not mean that the church is at peace with the world. There is a sense in which the church is in combat with the world that is within its own ranks and outside itself. About that we will say something in due time. But in our day perhaps the most serious struggle of the church is with that part of the world which has misunderstood it, that the church has, consciously and unconsciously, encouraged to adopt a spurious secularism which feigns worldliness, but is always showing its religious credentials. Such a secularism uses the church for its own purposes and, precisely for this reason, can believe that "religion is a good thing" as long as it is favorable to the *status quo*.

There is, however, an authentic secularism, singularly unpopular in religious America these days. It is critical of the church not so much because of what the church professes as because of its retreat from the struggle for freedom and justice, its fear of the truth whenever the truth does not correspond to its creed, its loss of the sense of the beauty and the terror of natural life. There are secularists who speak disparagingly of the church because they know very well what the Lordship of Christ means, but find themselves unable to accept the relationship between this Christ and the bland, middle-class Christianity which the church represents to them. Usually unawares, although sometimes quite consciously, they propagate the gospel and demonstrate its relevance in the idiom of the arts, the sciences, in the field of politics and human relations. They often misunderstand and distort the meaning of the faith, but despite themselves, some of these people are caught up in and used by the action of God for reconciliation.

One is sometimes struck with the amazing congruence between this secular understanding of the human situation, their passion for human freedom and justice, and that of prophetic Christianity. This is especially true in the field of literature, even taking into account the wide difference in quality between the writings of Albert Camus and the Beatnik poets of the North Beach in San Francisco. Even in Marxist circles, as distant as they are from a sympathetic view of Christianity, one can sometimes find the overtones of the deep humanity and openness toward the transcendent that clears the way for the gospel, preparing the ground for the seed, the silent growth, and finally the fruit of the Kingdom.

Johannes Hamel, a courageous witness to Christ in the East Zone of Germany, writes concerning a certain type of communist with whom he has contact: "This man who is so completely without religion . . . has a sensitive ear for the voice of the living God, who is the commander, judge, and rescuer of all. What happens in his encounter with Christians and pastors, quiet and hidden though it is, is the most important event of our days. Because here it becomes clear that there is no counterpower against the gospel, . . . that these estranged fanatics who seem to be at some quite different point stand in fact on the threshold of faith. Much, much closer to it than townsmen and farmers as long as they live undisturbed. The divine sword smashes tirelessly, even today, the ideological armor. If only Christians would take it in their hand!" ("Pfarrer in der Ostzone," in *Die neue Furche,* cited by Charles West, *Communism and the Theologians,* p. 280.)

It is difficult to describe this authentic secularism, partly because it is so evanescent. It comes and goes, and especially today, when it is surrounded by enemies, often disguises itself in the garb of spurious secularism. Every politician worth his salt knows how to make use of religious symbols and references in a campaign address. But the real difficulty in describing the attitude of authentic secularism is that there is a sense in which it is equal in honor and glory with true faith. It is hardly distinguishable from the secularity of authentic Christianity. It is in this sense that it makes room for the church and prepares the soil of the world for the gospel.

Let us now speak more specifically about this true or authentic secularism which corresponds in the world to what we have called true secularity in the church. By "authentic secularism" we refer to a sober, thisworldliness which, although it must always come short of true Christian realism, is nevertheless shaking off some of the illusions of our culture. And the greatest illusion from which this attitude has been liberated is that the man is essentially *homo religiosus* whose true home is somewhere other than this earth and whose noblest aspirations are set upon the things that are above rather than the things below. Certainly it is true that there is an underlying stratum of this "above and below" thinking in the New Testament. Since the Reformation, however, this thinking has not commended itself as the dominant motif of the Christian faith. It is there, but it has little significance today if by it we understand that kind of otherworldliness which precludes the secular relevance of the church.

Authentic secularism shares with Reformation Protestantism a certain empiricism about reality and existence.

When it is not idolatrous, it is a serious concern about the ordinary, the commonplace, the self-evident. It is an acceptance of the vitalities and realities of world existence as such, and for the autonomy of human life with all of the tragedy and creaturely joy that human freedom means.

This kind of secularism, though never found in pure form, is sometimes seen in the secular university, the theater, the art gallery, and in the day-to-day monotony of the practical politician and the harried social worker. It has its own role and responsibility in the strategy of redemption. Since it is not easily given to nonsense about man's basic needs in this world, it is in the places where action has to be waged for basic truth and justice often before the church arrives on the scene. It becomes, therefore, the important business of the church to look for this kind of secularism and to fight for it against the spurious secularism which desires and expects the church to be sentimental, mystical, and middle-of-the-road.

No one is better informed about the importance of this defensive action in behalf of realism than those who are today engaged in the struggle against hunger, colonialism, and racial segregation. Where the church has joined this struggle, it is aware that its most dangerous enemies are those benign secularists who talk about the "infiltration of communists" and "atheism" in order to alienate the church from people who may actually repudiate communism but nevertheless eschew gradualism and deny the superiority of Christian compassion over basic justice. In this connection it is important to note that, despite the early influence of Christian pacifism and nonviolence, many of the leaders of the student sit-ins, the main leadership of the Congress for Racial Equality and other movements for racial justice in the United States, are secularists who have been and are today most critical of the church and the social effects of religion. This does not mean that they have carried the main brunt of the struggle, nor have they been unaffected by the Christian witness of Martin Luther King and others. What has been accomplished in this country and abroad in the field of race relations represents, to a large degree, what is the most significant phenomenon of our generation—an *entente cordiale* between a realistic and militant Christianity and an authentic secularism. The Negro churches of Montgomery and the Christian missions in Africa and Asia that related the meaning of the revolution to the faith, laid the groundwork for this collaboration.

The church should realize that the people who talk about the moderating function of "religious values" and who give clergymen 20 per cent discounts are often the very people who are opposed to any real changes in our society for the amelioration and correction of social ills. For them nothing is very wrong with the society anyway. A five-hundred billion-dollar Gross National Product and rising business profits are excellent proof that free-enterprise economics and crowded churches make an unbeatable combination for success. The liberals, radicals, race agitators, and communist dupes ought to be driven out of the churches and sent to Russia, where they belong.

There are some churchmen who are not so easily taken in by this lip service to religion. They know that the index of the beatitude of this nation is not recorded exclusively in business statistics and that the main battle line of the churches is not in stained-glass foxholes, but on the ramparts of the world where a great cultural revolution is in process. They know that the theater of God's glory is not any other world than the world of the politician, the picket line, the East Harlem tenement, or the suburban Rotary meeting.

The true secularist also knows this world and what is wrong with it. He knows, sometimes better than Christians, that when this world is its true self, when it is most human, there is a glory that shines in it. He may not call this strange effulgence of the secular world the glory of God, but he may, nevertheless, sense that something has been given from the outside that transfigures the truly human life and bespeaks its ultimate meaning and destiny.

It is this sensitivity of the secularist to the ultimate significance which the secular itself radiates that gives the church its opportunity for dialogue. God is always bringing the secular man into a situation where this dialogue can be joined. He brings him face to face with ultimate concerns and final questions, which can make such a man surprisingly sensitive to the limits that have been placed around human existence. This can happen both when a man is borne to the pitch of exhilaration for the sheer joy of life, or when he stares bleakly into the face of death. But it also happens by the continuing witness of the church when the church, in dialogue or in proclamation by word and deed, manifests the action of God in the critique and reformation of the world. In this witness the world is affirmed and judged. The secularist cannot easily suppose that this affirmation and judgment do not concern him.

When Kerouac told the reporter, "I want God to show me his face," he was not merely quipping. This is the cry of an ultimate secularism, existing in its own right to be, despite itself, yoked to God's purposes. But it is ultimate and authentic secularism cracking under the judgment of the God who has shown his face in Jesus Christ, Savior of men. For that reason such a cry is not only a cry of unbelief, but a shout of creaturehood, a human cry that is authenticated and justified by the grace that comes to all men unceasingly and totally without merit.

This is secularism that has hope given to it by the grace of Christ. It is a true secularism in which God, sometimes through the indirect witness of the church and sometimes without, is already at work ministering to the world in order that it may be itself; in order that it may be faithful to its own reality, true to its own manner of existence as world—as *this* world—as man's world under the God who commands him to be free.

THE FALSE SECULARISM OF THE CHURCH

But let us now examine that other kind of secularism which has no hope but has many illusions—the secularism that is much more evident in American society today. We shall turn, therefore, to that spurious secularism which is so largely a creature of the church's faithlessness and its failure to find theological meaning for the secular in the cosmic Lordship of Christ.

H. B. Sissel tells the story of a Unitarian family in his suburban Philadelphia neighborhood that dared to publicly protest Bible-reading in the public school their children attended. From all over the nation the family received hate letters of the most blatant vulgarity. They were called "Jew Boys," "Communist bastards," "ungodly S.O.B.'s," and other choice epithets that suggest the Christian-democratic-100 per cent American self-image of the senders. Not a few of the letters closed with the words, "For God and country," or "In the name of our Lord and Savior, Jesus Christ."

Here is a striking example of the *affaire d'amour* between the American churches and the American culture that has spawned the illegitimate and highly ambiguous secularism of the greatest of all the "Christian" nations. This, we suggest, is really what the church must disaffiliate. It is not the secularism of the Beatniks and the "angry young men," the tongue-in-cheek journalists and positivistic social scientists, the power-drunk labor leaders, the A.D.A., and the Marxists. We have our problem with all of these; that is another problem for another essay. The real threat to the church and the relevance of its gospel to the world are the Christmas carols from November to January ringing down the shopper-filled streets, the Easter merchandising madness, the annual sally in the Congress to insert the name of Jesus Christ somewhere in the Constitution, the film versions of Biblical heroes who act like American suburbanites, the "Jesus Saves" billboards sponsored by an American Legion Post which is also persecuting the town librarian over "Red books for our children," the "Go to Church" posters with their customary portrayal of well-scrubbed, enrapt, prosperous-looking middle-class families—the one hundred and one, day-by-day subtle erasures of the line between the local church and the local country club, between Americanism and Christianity.

This is the demon who appears as an angel of light. We do not ordinarily think of it as secularism, and perhaps, generically, the word is inappropriate. But if there is a kind of worldliness based upon illusions, if there is a worldliness standing over against the realism of faith, it is this child of the unholy alliance between pietistic Christianity and patronizing Americanism. This is the secularism we should have feared.

What are some of the characteristics of this spurious secularism?—Its benevolent "godmothership" of the church by which it lavishes favors upon clergymen and the ecclesiastical institution as long as the public image is protected and the church does not have the ingratitude or indecency to cause a commotion. Its optimistic presuppositions about man who has, as one great corporation puts it, achieved "Better Living Through Chemistry" or will yet attain the motto that hangs over the stately portal of one Pennsylvania state college, "Wisdom, Truth, and Prosperity Through Education." Its Fourth of July speeches about "bringing America back to God" and "moral and spiritual values," which seem to add up to the vague suggestion that Americans should all be law-abiding citizens and go to the church of their choice. Its belief that the perfect formula for a young man's success in life is a college education, good grades in the physical sciences, an eye for business, and just enough religion to be esteemed by respectable people.

This kind of secularism escapes unnoticed because it is subliminal. It is so bland, so inoffensive to the Christian conscience. No one can say very much against it because whatever may be its deficiencies in terms of integrity and cogency, it works. It has undergirded and given direction to a society that has the most idealistic aspirations, the most humane sympathies, the most generous pocketbook, and the highest standard of living in the world today. What could be wrong with it? With the exception of a few slowdowns and a few temporary stoppages, it has worked since the middle of the nineteenth century and it will continue to work miracles of affluence, pride, and religiosity.

Perhaps the most striking feature of this kind of secularism is that it is basically fearful and conservative. It rests upon illusion rather than hope. It will applaud steady progress as long as balances are not upset. But it fears any motion, either forward or backward, that would threaten the comfort and security of the moment. Its interest, therefore, is in "more and more of the same" and in the stability that this supposedly guarantees. Any religion or political philosophy that threatens to undo the matter-of-fact, automatic control and organization of life, any group that promotes social radicalism and nonconformity, is under suspicion of being either terroristic and fanatical or the dupes of some foreign conspiracy.

This false secularism, for all its religiosity, is afraid of passion. Everything must remain quiet. The *status quo* must be preserved at all costs. It must hold everything on even keel. It wants to relate persons to each other, integrate their personalities, meet their needs, socialize their children, plan their communities, and preserve their democratic rights and property values in the most reasonable and efficient manner possible. The churches can and must help the society to accomplish these enlightened objectives. They may—indeed, they are expected—occasionally to prick the social conscience or to remonstrate mildly about this way of doing things or that; but they must not cross the boundary of propriety, aspire to power, organize resistance, apply sanctions, or do anything that affronts the remembrance of gentle Jesus and frustrates the smoothly functioning apparatus which has thrust the nation to the present level of economic security and social integration.

So it is that despite all the talk about adult education for grass-roots democracy, encouraging individual initiative and citizen participation, rationalization and routinization have become characteristic of a society dominated by the false secularism. Life becomes a guided tour in which everyone is properly identified, in step, and happily (if possible) serving the interests of those who really have the power to implement decisions. This secularism is false because for all of its worldly concerns, it is not worldly enough. It is not authentic secularism. It is only the moralistic and ideological consensus of the American middle class or of those who aspire to that class, carefully prodded and patronized by businessmen and politicians, and made slightly aromatic by the elusive perfume of Christianity.

American society today is nurtured by quite a different kind of secularism than that which has shown a surprising ability to liberate itself from conventional illusions and ideologies and the great myths of the rural past and has a new and painful sensitivity to an inexorable judgment that it recognizes as coming from Somewhere outside of itself. The curious situation in which we find ourselves is that it is the spurious secularism, so comfortable and happy with the church, which threatens true secularism and true faith. On the other hand, the true secularism—the basic humanistic passion for truth, justice, and freedom—is the possession of marginal persons and groups that are today largely estranged from the church.

It is this paradoxical and threatening condition of contemporary American society that gives the church its "fighting situation," to use the striking phrase of Don Matthews, the "minister in industry" at Kalamazoo, Michigan. It calls the church to make alliances with strange comrades-in-arms in a war against secularism in behalf of a deeper secularity. It calls the church to political and cultural action, not in order to assume a permanent leadership and control of the society, but as its most stringent critic, to blast its illusions and make it face unblinkingly the responsibility to be itself, to undertake the hard and human work of building a society of free men on the craggy shores of reality, pummeled by the limitless ocean of eternity and swept by the winds of God.

If the church undertakes this fight, it will find that allies will come from the most unexpected places. Not every man who plays his cards when his turn comes is satisfied with the game. From the lonely, marginal people of the great cities, from the racial and cultural subcommunities, from among the disillusioned of the underprivileged classes and the cynical of the middle classes, from among the tired liberals and the melancholy intelligensia, from the new masses of Africa, Asia, and Latin America—from all of these and from other places where we least expected to find friends, allies will come forward to hear and heed the gospel and take up the work of rebuilding the world. God is moving today in hidden ways among all these groups. If the church understands and accepts the true secularity of its calling, it will meet him in their midst. Perhaps in that day we will hear with new meaning the words of Jesus concerning that lonely secularist, the Roman centurion: "Truly, I say to you, not even in Israel have I found such faith. I tell you, many will come from east and west and sit at table with Abraham, Isaac, and Jacob in the kingdom of heaven, while the sons of the kingdom will be thrown into outer darkness" (Matt. 8:10–12).

Chapter III
The Faithful Use of Power

The politics of change, whether seen as orderly revolution or as an armed upheaval, is not choosing abrupt change over a more desirable evolutionary change. The unwarranted introduction of the evolutionary idea into social and political thinking has been a deceiving curse. Societies do not evolve. They do not obey unconscious laws of their own nature. They are the deliberate creations of men. They change when men decide to change them. The changes are not always wise or even understood by the changers, but what happens is the outcome of conscious, purposeful action.—Nicholas von Hoffman, in an unpublished paper, "Reorganization in the Casbah."

Christians take for granted that the God who has revealed himself through Jesus Christ is active in the world through the power by which he sustains, uproots, and transforms men and nations. The Christian God is not a Cosmic Machinist. The world, for all the appearances of it, is not some great machine running on interminably with millions of large and small gears meshing in an infinitely intricate synchronization. We believe that the laws of nature which make life possible and which hold the planets in orbit operate from millennium to millennium at the behest of a Creator-Judge-Redeemer, who is also involved in the ebb and flow of human history.

Not only does he continually uphold the laws of the natural order, but by his sovereign will and purpose, by his manifest power, he judges and redeems, restrains and directs, the processes of human events.

Against every attempt to pick God out from the husk of the world, as one picks the kernel from a nut, against every effort to eject God from the cockpit of his world, the Christian church makes this confession of his living presence and his sovereign power. By his word and will, the world is created, judged, and redeemed, and this not "once upon a time," but in this place and at this time and for all time to come.

"For as the rain and the snow come down from heaven, and return not thither but water the earth, making it bring forth and sprout, giving seed to the sower and bread to the eater, so shall my word be that goes forth from my mouth; it shall not return to me empty, but it shall accomplish that which I purpose, and prosper in the thing for which I sent it." (Isa. 55:10–11.)

The black banner headlines in the morning paper speak of the power and the action of God as surely as do the words of the prophets and the New Testament witnesses. Notwithstanding the fact that there is no easy formula for knowing how and to what immediate ends God is moving in the restless flux of happenings, the Christian confesses that the hand of God is behind, within, and against whatever transpires in the universe. He seeks, therefore, to discern, through the binoculars of faith, what it is precisely that God is doing to accomplish that which pleases him and then to join him at that place and time with the human instrumentalities at his disposal.

It is difficult for us to believe in the *living* God. Most of us read the newspapers like unbelievers because, despite all the Easter sermons, we have restricted God to the period during which the Bible was written. But the history of our time is no less the stage upon which the drama of salvation is played out than was the history of the fifth century B.C. or the first century A.D. Accordingly, the Christian does not doubt that God is moving with power in the world today—the world of African nationalism, thermonuclear politics, metropolitan planning, and space exploration. The Christian's problem is rather to discover when, where, and how God is moving with such decisiveness as to create a crisis of decision for the church and to summon it and its resources into the struggle.

The problem is to read the signs of the time, wherever signs are available. One of the supper club comedians quips that the new middle-class Negro commutes to Manhattan every morning with *The Wall Street Journal* under one arm and *Ebony* magazine under the other. The Christian similarly, with the Bible and a good newspaper, strides out into the world to work. It is not so simple a matter that in one he finds faith and in the other fact. It is rather because of who he is and because of the community of faith to which he belongs, he needs both the Bible and a reasonably accurate record of contemporary events—the trick being to read one between the lines of the other. It is by means of both of these "resources" that he comes to know who he is and the truth of his situation in the buzzing, busy, ever-shifting scene before his view.

What does the Christian see when he tries to make sense of the events of today in terms of what he has learned from Christ? William H. Whyte, Jr., discussing the change from Western society of the eighteenth century, which saw the individual as a separate and autonomous unit, to the organized society of the twentieth century, speaks of the "social ethic" as "that contemporary body of thought which makes morally legitimate the pressures of society against the individual." Certainly one of the ubiquitous characteristics of present reality is the great shift of power from the individual to the group, and the pressures accompanying it. This shift began during the

Industrial Revolution and has greatly accelerated in our own day. The clan, the tribe, or the group had for many ages been an important segment of humanity. The important difference between the group in former years and today is its contractual and bureaucratic formation today. The rationalization of group life and the quasi-legal alignment of one group with another becomes one of the requirements and effects of a technological civilization.

In the communist societies, group membership and participation is frequently the result of overt and legitimatized coercion, as in the Siberian labor camps, the farm collectives, and the Chinese village communes. A more subtle form of coercion operates in the democratic West. In all our basic industries, and in an increasing number of secondary and tertiary pursuits, to belong to a group, a labor union or a manufacturers' or trade association, is not a simple matter of personal prerogative. Membership in a particular political party (or nonmembership in certain political parties), inclusion as a member of a group in certain kinds of tax obligations and other levies, conformity to certain status requirements and community standards, which are no longer matters of individual taste and judgment, are as necessary for normal operation and the realization of certain personal ends in American society as they are in the Soviet Union. In our case, the pressure on the individual toward participation in a collectivity may be more disguised and subtle. It is no less real. At times, as in periods of feverish preparation for national defense, it is overt and unabashed.

The Influence of Voluntary Associations

In the United States we can still refer to most of our collective involvements with the euphemism of "voluntary associations" because there is a considerable area of activity in which one may elect to take the consequences of nonparticipation without experiencing severe sanctions. Here voluntary associations, which exist mainly among the middle classes, provide a means by which individuals can "improve themselves," or "do something" about their feelings of anxiety and rootlessness. Obviously many people in our country join groups for this purpose. In a real sense they volunteer for the value orientation and psychological security a group provides.

But many others in the United States become members and actively participate in collectivities because they want to maintain or increase their economic and political power. Even ostensibly "social groups"—fraternal and recreational organizations—have latent functions connected with political or business interests. A study of the power structure of a small Midwestern community conducted by the author revealed that several of the leading men felt that they had to play cards at the Elks Club certain nights of the week if they wanted to protect their business interests. Some of the most important deals of the community were made around the poker table at the Elks. Although this group was "voluntary," it was only voluntary, in any meaningful sense, for those who had so much power that they were unaffected by the group's decisions (and these people were often represented by proxies) or for those who had so little that the group's decisions seemed irrelevant to their interests.

When one considers the network of groups—economic, social, political, cultural, religious—in the United States today, how they proliferate from local to regional to national levels of affiliation, and how they concentrate and centralize power, one begins to understand the sense in which John R. Commons observes that we live in an "age of collective action." Few decisions of importance to the lives of individuals, few events, occur in the nation that are not conceived and carried out by organized groups. Kenneth Boulding, in *The Organizational Revolution,* writes that there are some 250,000 voluntary groups in the United States that hold about 15,000 annual state and national conventions. He calls these, mainly "philanthropic" organizations, "the third level of the American power structure," following in order, government and business. When the network of groups in the governmental, military, business, and industrial subsystems of the society are added to the voluntary groups of Boulding's description, the full significance of group decision and activity in this society becomes disturbingly evident.

Arthur S. Miller, in a paper on the role of the corporation in the free society, points out that in orthodox constitutional theory nothing intermediate between the government and the individual person is envisaged. Not even the political party is recognized in the Federal Constitution. To persist in the fiction that the term "collective" applies only to those societies which are under the totalitarianism of communist domination is to ignore one of the most pervasive features of modern life. Between formal governmental authority and the individual are massive congeries of organized power that provides the control and functional basis for modern democratic society.

We might mention only a few widely separated and diverse groups to suggest the broad expanse of life that comes within their purview: the National Association of Manufacturers, the three largest farm organizations, the AFL–CIO, the political parties, the press, radio, and TV associations, the League of Women Voters, the various health and welfare organizations, the veterans groups, the hundreds of philanthropic foundations, the National Association for the Advancement of Colored People, the American Medical Association, the National Education Association, the scouting groups and the national recreational and travel organizations. Many more and equally influential groups could be mentioned, but the point is obvious. These "voluntary" associations, through their subsidiary bodies that reach into every city, town, and village, into every home, church, and school in the nation, largely determine the ethos of American society.

These countless collectivities give us our images of ourselves, our impressions of others, our prides and prejudices, our myths and traditions, our tastes and preferences, our values and attitudes about everything from loyalty to God and country to kindness to dumb animals. They give Americans their peculiar folkways and mores, their public behavior and private opinions, the patterns of their social skills and know-how about everything, from building a family fallout shelter to performing the latest dance step. The decisions that a man makes about where he will live, how he will furnish his home (the women's magazines, of course, will make this decision in co-operation with the furniture manufacturers), how he will discipline his children, what radio and TV commentators he will listen to, what newspapers and magazines he will subscribe to, and what organizations he will join in his community—all of these daily decisions are, to an inestimable but unquestionable degree, influenced by the legislation, education, and plain ballyhoo daily propagated by these groups and the power centers that control them.

We must stop now to ask the inevitable question. Where are the churches in all of this? Is there any sense in which they belong to this "third level of the American power structure," which is mixed up in the collection of influences we have described?

Since the organization of the National Catholic Welfare Conference in 1919, the Roman Catholic Church in this country, consistent with its own understanding of the relation between the church and American culture, has been soberly aware of the role and responsibility it bore with respect to this configuration of power. Where Roman Catholics were deeply involved, as in the trade-union movement or in the question of aid to parochial schools, the hierarchy has used every point of influence and organizational facility to protect its own interests. Where its traditional support of natural law and concern for the "common good" was the point of its entry into the public sphere, as in the issue of desegregation in the South and urban planning in the North, the Roman Catholic Church has not failed to make open statements of its position and to use its moral influence to encourage orderly change.

The picture is very similar for the Protestant Church. But at three points there are noteworthy differences. First of all, the Protestant churches, although they officially support the doctrine of the wall of separation between church and state, have never been able to perceive a clear demarcation between the church and the culture. Law has defined the separation in principle, but practice varies. The Protestant churches assumed, therefore, that the ethos of the nation, so greatly influenced by associational groupings in which their own members were in majority, was unambiguously a Protestant ethos. And so it seemed. The question today is whether what has been assimilated into the culture of many groups and associations that might one day have been expressions of authentic Protestantism, such as the Young Men's Christian Association or the Grange, has not now evaporated. In many of these groups, not necessarily the two mentioned, what is left is a curious blend of religion and secularism that we have identified with "Main Street Morality," free-enterprise Americanism, or the sociopolitical privatism and isolationist tendencies of ruralism and the American Right.

A second difference grows out of the first. The American Protestant churches have always been either dominated by laymen or by professional clergy extremely sensitive to the powerful lay constituency and orientation of the churches. Protestant laymen, in positions of ecclesiastical power or in *de facto* control of those who were, have been fearful of secular power. For them the countinghouse is not the meetinghouse and there ought to be no confusion betwen the functions and limitations of each. It has become clear, of course, that it is much easier to restrict the functions and define the limitations of the meetinghouse than the countinghouse. But the fact is that the adage "religion and politics don't mix" has been the basic cultural assumption of Protestant laity. Getting rid of the liquor industry and houses of prostitution, or "throwing the rascals out" of a corrupt city hall were actions never seen clearly as examples of the church meddling in politics. These were "moral issues" well within the province of religion and as soon as they were settled, as soon as local hegemony was returned to the "decent, respectable people" of the community, the churches exhibited little interest in power-wielding or in maintaining a continuing relationship to public affairs. "A kind word, a warm smile, and a hearty handshake," wrote one spokesman in a national Protestant magazine, is more effective for church strategy in race relations than all of its social and political action programs. This is a typical Protestant response to the question of how God is acting in a crisis situation and what is the church's responsibility for power.

The third difference is that the Protestant Church, to a much greater degree than the Roman Catholic Church, is divided sociologically and theologically. This has made a considerable difference in its approach to organized power in public affairs. Councils and federations of churches struggle against the institutional centrism of local churches and denominations. They represent today the barest minimum of Protestant consensus across confessional lines. Although undoubtedly there is considerably more Protestant co-operation in overseas and home missions today than ever before, the churches have found it possible to do very little together in the field of social policy and social action beyond agreeing on "major areas of concern." The nationwide storm that arose among the laity as a result of the National Council of Churches Cleveland Study Conference report in 1959 on the feasibility of working toward the time when Red China could take its place in the United Nations is a classic example of the slender thread upon which Protestant leaders hang when they attempt to present a united front on a controversial public policy question.

When one considers the Protestant indecision about its cultural role, its long-standing disinclination to resort to secular means to achieve goals upon which there may be considerable agreement, and the great difficulty the churches have in reaching that agreement and legitimizing its expression in public pronouncement and action, the result is a picture of the stalemate in which Protestantism stands with respect to increasing its influence in the American power structure.

Nevertheless, Protestant churches are unquestionably members of the voluntary group level to which we have alluded. Sociologists have long emphasized the integrative role the churches play in relation to primary groups like the family and how they cultivate and support the basic value system of the society. But church participation in the crucial decisions facing the society as it moves into "the age of collective action" has been more by accident than by deliberate intent. Something of Protestantism has assuredly "rubbed off" on the decision makers, and it has not always been the best, the most distinctive contribution of the Reformation. This was obvious when former President Truman averred that his foreign policy was based upon the Sermon on the Mount. Very little has been consciously and effectively "inserted" into the society. And that which is projected in this way is quickly demarcated and labeled as sectarian, denominational, and essentially of secondary importance to the over-all secular concern.

The consequence of all this has been highly ambiguous, to say the least. On one hand, the church, by its refusal or inability to consolidate policy and institutionalize its involvement in the shaping of significant areas of life, has appeared to have assumed a genuine posture of secularity. There is a sense in which it has seemed to recognize that God was able to act through powers other than those of the church. To this extent it has been true to its earliest heritage and expressed confidence in the value and relative autonomy of the secular enterprise. On the other hand, the church has demonstrated a naïve and moralistic approach to social reality. It has assumed that if it eschewed power its "social concern" would have an educative influence and its massive institutional baggage would at least not give either side of a struggle an advantage as long as it remained a "nonpolitical" factor in the social order. It has been wrong on both counts. And when, on rare occasions, it has acted as a national power group committed to a certain course of action, it has shown a singular ineffectiveness. Its retirement into enclaves of decency for the socialization and protection of its own constituency has been more characteristic of its understanding of the relationship between the church and the culture than any consistent appreciation of the secular or attempts to be relevant to it.

What is the situation today? There is little evidence that Protestantism is beginning to clarify its image of itself in the direction of a more active participation in collective decision-making. Indeed, there are some signs that both American Protestantism and Roman Catholicism are moving in the opposite direction. If the influence of religious affiliation and pulpit exhortation upon voting patterns is any index of power potential when church interests are implicated in a struggle, neither communion demonstrated anything remarkable in the presidential election of 1960. In comparison with socioeconomic status, church membership is inconsiderable in most American elections.

There is, nevertheless, no abatement in the number and frequency of church pronouncements, policy statements, and studies that express righteous indignation about mounting crime statistics, racial discrimination, the problems of the city, and the drift toward World War III. It would appear, therefore, that the Protestant churches, despite the loss of their former ascendancy, still think of themselves as having an authoritative and effective voice in public affairs. Certainly their professional leaders hold out the hope that the churches will become still more influential and take a more active role in the formulation of the national purpose and the achievement of social goals.

Are Protestants ready to accept the full implication of this understanding of the cultural vocation of the church in terms of participation in public policy formation? We wonder. The belief that any application of power by the church is a betrayal of the love ethic of the gospel and the most precious traditions of democratic society lies deep in the soul of American Protestantism. This belief must be subjected to searching theological analysis and some necessary modification. Certainly any aspirant to an effective role in American society today must take two facts of life with the utmost seriousness. First, the reality of socioeconomic structures of power that institutionalize and "regularize" decision-making in every area of modern life. There may be ways of bypassing these structures. But let us not be deceived. Political, economic, and social organizations and interests have a way of disguising themselves within the "nonpolitical," informal ways decisions are made.

Second, the necessity, in most instances, of consolidated policy and corporate action to effect change or to influence the social system to any considerable extent.

Policy, in the sense in which we are using it, is "political" or more precisely, the bid for political power. We are using the words "policy" and "political" broadly, as any decision by any group or organization that can be calculated to influence the attitudes or actions of people outside of itself. In this sense, the decision of the Master Barbers' Association to open neighborhood shops until church time on Sundays is just as surely political policy as an ordinance passed by the city council.

It is possible to exaggerate the notion of "power elites" and structures of determinative power and influence in important areas of American society. Many church leaders on the local and regional levels, however, still make policy without the least awareness of its effect or lack of *desirable* effect upon the social, economic, and political structures. Official boards still vote to keep a church open or to relocate a congregation without sufficient attention either to the consequence of such decisions or to countervailing decisions by planning bodies, industries, or important social groupings. Today the major denominations are more wary of the implications of social structure, but mainly at the headquarters level. And their decisions cannot be consistently enforced in the field. In many smaller denominations little or nothing is being done in this regard. Many church groups conduct programs of "public affairs" as if persons are autonomous units, isolated from the influence of power entities in their communities and able to regulate their behavior under all circumstances by dint of sheer moral will.

A group of Presbyterian elders who were also realtors in a Pittsburgh community were asked by their pastor to open the way for a cultured Negro family to purchase a home in their neighborhood. After a lengthy discussion in which they consulted Scripture, prayed, and generally agonized over a decision, they summoned their minister and reported: "Our duty is clear. We know that as

Christian men we ought to give the word that would make it possible for this man to find a house here, but, God help us, we cannot do it. Most of us have spent a lifetime building up our businesses. The reprisals from the realty board, the banks, and certain other groups would be more than we could take and stay in business. Not only our businesses but our families would suffer all kinds of threats and social ostracism. We just can't do what we know we ought to do as Christians."

The call to obedience always is a call to deny oneself and to suffer with Christ. No one can relieve these men of the guilt and shame of their unfaithfulness to what they saw as an imperative of the gospel. Only Christ himself can absolve them. And yet, no one can fail empathically to brood over the realities of this situation, the inevitability and rigidity of the institutional sanctions to which these "good" men were pitilessly exposed. To expect people lightly to make choices without respect to the contexts of power in which they have to live and work is to delude ourselves with pious hopes. The church has a responsibility here to demonstrate a corporate fellowship of love and power that is able both to uphold these men in forgiveness and to point the way to an obedience for which the church itself is willing to suffer. Unless the church can be responsible enough to the reality of an organized society, and faithful enough to use the economic and cultural power of its own to change the situation, it cannot be indignant if most laymen, much less if people outside the church, find it impossible to do what they feel morally obligated to do.

The research of sociologists Joseph D. Lohman and D. C. Reitzes on the behavior of individuals toward Negroes as affected by their participation in "interest groups" and other sociological investigations of group pressures indicate the power of organized groups, especially where social prestige and economic interests are involved. People tend to define their situations in terms of the norms of the groups in which they are most deeply involved and which are most relevant to their daily life. This means that the groups which have power and use it in the most important areas of life will—unless they overextend themselves—achieve the greater discipline and loyalty, Radio Free Europe and the West Berlin showcase notwithstanding. It is greatly to the misfortune of the churches that they have helped successfully to restrict the province of religion to the socialization of children, affability, and the sphere of individual morals and beliefs. Many other groups are not so handicapped. The spheres of their power interests impinge upon some of the crucial areas of a person's life. When the requirements of participation and the definitions of life situations that are promulgated by these groups are not seriously challenged, middle-class religious institutions are no match for them.

In so far as people in our culture act in segmentalized roles as defined and required by organized groups able to apply social and economic power, the church that makes no demands upon its members, gives them no stronghold from which to fight, and is afraid to use its own institutional power when it is necessary is simply eliminated from the struggle. It leaves a power vacuum to be filled by organized interests made up of the church's own bewildered members. It abandons the field to communism on the left and Birchism on the right.

The church may, because it takes the secular with utmost seriousness, permit this to happen without becoming unduly anxious about its own institutional life. But it will hopefully determine under what conditions and to what ends it will defer to other groups. It is precisely because it regards the secular seriously that the church will be aware of the structures of collective power and will seek to change them in order to make room for the gospel, and to take some share in the determination of individual and group behavior in the critical spheres of modern life.

There appear to be no real alternatives. It is a question of fishing or cutting bait. It is not a matter of the church's trying to do what political parties and great corporations are better equipped to do. That would be both impossible and undesirable. It is simply a matter of the church's doing what is possible for it in each situation; to use faithfully that modicum of power it can generate and call a halt to the retreat from the firing line and the pious pretension that God works only through the weak and powerless.

Consolidated Policy and Corporate Action

We have now come to the place where we must speak more specifically about what we mean by consolidated policy and corporate action by the church. These terms have a hard, bureaucratic ring—like a hammer on cold steel. One does not feel them in the way one feels words such as "Christian fellowship," "moral example," and "sacrificial love," all of which seem to be more appropriate ways to speak of the strategy of reconciliation. Could such terms as "consolidated policy" and "corporate action" have anything to do with a gospel about the living God who acts where and as he will, or with a church that teaches men to make up their minds, take up their cross, and follow Jesus?

Let us be clear about the fact that individuals can and do "change the world." At a strategic time one man with an idea and enough determination and skill to see it through, can accomplish much even under a rigidly totalitarian system. From Moses in Egypt to Vinoba Bhave in India—neither of whom, we might note incidentally, was Christian—God has chosen occasionally to use a single individual to accomplish great reforms. This truth should make the church exceedingly careful never to sever the nerve of individual action. We should consider, however, if it is not also true that God has more often used two or three or twelve or ten thousand, and if, in an organized, power-wielding society, it is not a matter of urgency that Christians consolidate their positions and undertake united action on certain issues of public concern.

By a consolidation of public policy we refer to something more than a general consensus among the church public that this or that thing would be good for the neighborhood or the nation. There is already an appreciable measure of Protestant consensus about generalities. The consolidation of policy rather refers to unifying varied points of view about technological development, the nature of community, the meaning of the material world, the regulative norms and goals of a secular society. It refers to a unified conception of some long-range cultural goals, some immediate objectives, and the specific means by which to seek them. It has finally to do with agreements about what the church ought to do in the society, when and how, and the allocation of resources and the co-ordination of forces to put proposals into action. Again the matter-of-fact, cold-blooded way we have stated these policy questions does not mean that they have to be cold and mechanical either in consideration or execution. These things cannot properly be programed for an IBM machine. We are talking about people—meeting, planning, working, in the mission of the church in the real world in which we live today and must live, with millions of new and unfamiliar peoples, in the future.

By corporate action, we refer simply to "acting as a body." This may involve the official, authorized action of a congregation or of a delegated group in behalf of a congregation; or action by a group of churches or by that delegated body that is able to act in their behalf. It will be clear, therefore, that by corporate action we mean to imply action as an organized power group which may not be able to deliver all that it promises in the way of effective power, but which has, nevertheless, some of the resources and some of the institutional weight of a corporate entity behind it.

This rather naked description of church corporate action should not frighten us merely because of the words "organized," "power," and "institutional." Every church and every assemblage of churches has institutional characteristics, power, and organization. The important ethical questions concern not their existence but how they are put together and used. These questions cannot be ignored by the Christian church if it intends to be relevant in the world to which it has been sent. The existence of difficult ethical questions in a given situation need not preclude our speaking frankly of the organization of the legitimate institutional power of the church for effective action in the world.

Nor does corporate action exclude individual action or action in collaboration with other individuals or groups outside the church. When laymen are asked to take responsibility in certain community groups and to report back to the congregation, as in the Church of the Savior in Washington, D.C., or as the Church Federation of Chicago sends representatives to the Citizen School Committee which provides a list of candidates for the school board, that is a kind of corporate action, carried out by individuals. When the Presbytery of Detroit takes out a Life Membership in the National Association for the Advancement of Colored People, thereby lending its name to and sharing in the control of that organization, that is also a kind of corporate action. A small Negro congregation in Laurinburg, North Carolina, engaged in a form of corporate action when a delegation, led by the minister, presented the manager of a local supermarket with statistics on the number of Negro shoppers using the store and persuaded him to adopt a fair employment policy. In New York City a committee of women representing a national church organization held a secret meeting with dime-store executives about opening lunch counters in the South. In Tulsa a group of ministers and members of their congregations organized an auxiliary police group and succeeded in forcing the city police department to rid itself of corruption. All of these, with various strengths and weaknesses, represent forms of corporate action.

Most of what the churches have demonstrated in corporate action has been in the area of race relations, but more could have been done in other areas. In the next chapter we will examine one example of church corporate action that is relevant to a broad expanse of problems in a complex metropolitan community. This form of action is not absent in the Protestant churches today. The idea of organizing and caucusing for the purpose of influencing persons and groups outside the church is not generally regarded as contrary to the purpose and mission of the church. The problem is to bring many laymen to face the implications of this strategy and to increase its effectiveness within organized social and political life. There has, admittedly, been some confusion. Corporate action does not mean that "everyone agrees and everyone goes." It can mean quasi-official representation. It simply means bringing to bear upon a situation as much united power as can be organized, with the result that something is moved or inhibited outside the acting group.

The old question of the difficulty of achieving consolidated policy and corporate action in the Protestant churches has been somewhat exaggerated. One would have to admit that it is always difficult, and on highly controversial issues, almost impossible. But we must wonder whether our methods of introducing and dealing with issues has not been the main source of difficulty. Protestant leaders have too often been bound by their own sentimental notions about the "grass roots" and the ethics of decision-making. The assumption that "if it doesn't happen in the local church, it doesn't happen," for all its good intentions to maintain that the locus of Christianity is in the pews, is certainly not consonant with the structural nature of the society and of the churches. Such thinking is still geared to an individualistic, "popular government" image of the church, which no longer, or rarely, corresponds to reality.

The fact is that, for good or ill, many things happen in terms of the mission of the church that do not happen "in the local church." Funds are invested, agreements entered into, studies made, pronouncements delivered, projects executed on regional and area levels. This is the way a modern, bureaucratic organization operates, and the denominations—we may as well admit it—are no exceptions. It is taken for granted, though rarely acknowledged publicly, that most people on the local level—the Sunday morning congregations—are neither sufficiently interested nor organized to make it feasible to secure their approval or personal involvement in some of the most important actions of the church.

This is not to imply that these people are not the church. Nor are we disparaging the local congregation and the individual church member. All of us have important responsibilities and competences within the limited context of the actual congregation where our membership is held. No one can deny, moreover, the necessity of raising the level of commitment and involvement on the part of individual members of local congregations in the affairs of their own communities. We will later make some suggestions toward the strengthening of the usual way in which this is done. But it is unrealistic and injurious to the effective witness of the church to suppose that we cannot act without unanimity or without clearing with whole constituencies. Granting that ethical problems are involved in "steam-roller tactics" and "administrative decisions," the fact remains that the structures of most of the leading Protestant denominations provide ample opportunity for more effective social action than executives have thought possible.

Our problem is not that the church would fall apart if a bold attempt were made by its leaders to consolidate policy and use corporate action in some highly controversial area. Despite the fact that some much-needed pruning of dead branches might be the result of such an eventuality, a permanent split in a congregation is not so likely to occur as most pastors fear. Our problem is rather the persistent illusion that the modern church should operate like a New England town meeting and does in fact so operate on all important issues. Our problem is the somewhat pharisaical—in the light of the way most church bodies are run—repudiation of "church politics" and the failure of nerve to press for a united position among effective members or agencies for that measure of corporate action possible in a given situation.

Even in church federations and councils, where the problem of policy-making and united action is sometimes very difficult, much more can be done by those who are willing to move. The responsible use of institutional power requires that many factors be taken into consideration in the estimation of probable consequences, but people who are politically and sociologically equipped, as well as theologically informed, will take calculated risks that can strengthen the influence of the church in their communities.

Let us hasten to insist that this is no invitation to power-hungry church executives to join in an amoral play of power politics within the churches. The political astuteness and the humility of Lincoln were not incompatible qualities of his character. We must be aware of our pretensions and of the temptations to infallibility. But the mission of the church in today's world is a serious business. It demands savvy, skill, and faithfulness to use power in such a way as to rout the wolves without killing the sheep. The church will not save the world. But if it has any message for modern man, if it has any place for him to stand and fight against the demoralizing and tyrannizing structures of a culture that has been severed from its true secular responsibility to serve human need, then those Christians who know this must speak and act. They cannot falter before the hard decision to employ responsibly the power and prestige of the church to help it become the catalyst by which the culture can fulfill its obligation for the humanization of the life of man.

We began this chapter by enunciating the Christian confession that God, as Creator-Judge-Redeemer, is active in the world. Let us also confess that no Christian nor organization of Christians is wise enough to know precisely what God is doing in every situation. But this much we can say with confidence: at every point of suffering and wrong, in every situation where man is being divested of his essential humanity, the judgment and the grace of God is operative through some human agency. The church of Christ is not called merely to be a spectator to this drama of reconciliation. The church must make decisions about "what is going on" even when this is not clear. It must be willing to fight, even when most of its members prefer to go fishing.

The missionary church has a variety of postures. At one time it will stand silently in the midst of the world, waiting to hear more clearly the accents of the Lord of the world. But it ought not to fall asleep while it waits for a message. The Word, by which it is able to declare "Thus saith the Lord," has already been given to it. Therefore, it will also say "yes" here and "no" there in the assurance that, like Abraham, God has called it to go in faith, and has given the church—let Protestants also be bold enough to say—as *mater et magistra* to all the families of the earth.

We shall have been grossly misunderstood if all this suggests the pre-Reformation church, proud and infallible, weighted down with secular authority, dreaming of transforming the world into "one great Sunday school." The responsibility of the church for power does not mean bidding for sovereignty over the structures and institutions of society. It means penetrating them in such a way as to be able to instruct the world concerning its purpose of serving human need, concerning its original foundation and the end toward which it moves. It means so energizing these structures and institutions, within their own provinces and with the spirit appropriate to their own function, that they can act as the true creatures of God they are. To perform this task today requires the faithful use of power. This ministry is not forbidden to the church by its Lord. For the church does not serve obsequiously—a flunky, bowing and scraping with hat in hands—but rather as the sophisticated English butler who has more brains, is more of a gentleman, and has more resources for helping his "master" become a real man than the master can muster for himself.

If God is a living God, he is acting in the world through the existing apparatus for getting things done; his "livingness" is not antithetical to life as we know it. The organized church is a part of this apparatus and the institutional power it possesses has the legitimate function of placing it in the spheres where God is at work. This power is far from being a sinful possession, a hindrance to the reconciling activity of God. Rather, power is his gift to the church in order that, with a due sense of humility and a prudent appreciation of its demonic possibilities, it may be used faithfully to the glory of God.

It makes no sense for the church to disclaim power or to refuse to use it responsibly when occasion demands. It is a fact of human existence, and dramatically so in modern society. It is, in the sociological sense, the ability to affect another person, consciously or unconsciously, with or without his consent, through one's own action or inaction. It is a concept related to the deep interpenetration of one life with another. As Walter Wiest has said, "Power is strikingly reminiscent of the definition of the 'neighbor' in the Christian sense as anyone whose welfare is affected by what I do or fail to do." Already the implication for the Christian use of power begins to emerge in virtue of the inseparable relationship between "powerhood" and "neighborhood" in the organized society of today.

Let us acknowledge that we tread on slippery ground. The divine power of God is not precisely the earthly power of the church. That question was settled in the Reformation. But the action of God and the power-wielding of the church must somehow be made to cohere. This is not an easy task in any case, and there is always the possibility that God will repudiate the power of his church today as he did in the Reformation, the Russian revolution, and in the American disestablishment of religion. That is his sovereign prerogative. Especially in the United States, where there is an old suspicion of ecclesiastical power in secular affairs, the strategy of Christian action proposed here may never be tolerated. In this event, once again the voice of the people may be the voice of God.

But let us not leap too quickly to conclusions about what the American people will do in these perilous times, or what the church may be able to do with serpentine wisdom and the harmlessness of doves. It will indeed test the wisdom and the love of Protestantism so to prove its servantship to the culture, so to use its power for the freedom and the enhancement of life, that the American people, as well as other peoples of the world, will not only welcome this new agency of responsibility but bless the God who sends it into the world as his witness.

Chapter IV

The Equipment of the Saints

Whatever we call the small group I am talking about—this second focus of our life as a congregation—it must have as a strenuous emphasis preparing its members for the concrete tasks which they face outside the life of the colony. It must not be designed to make us more pious or simply to instill more knowledge about our faith. That has the effect of insulating us from the world or compartmentalizing our religious interest. The small group, as well as the corporate life of the church, exists not to stimulate or create koinonia but to prepare us for the mission of the church.—George W. Webber, *God's Colony in Man's World.*

We have described the peculiar situation in which American Protestantism finds itself with its heritage of individualism in an age of tremendous organized pressures. By means of a sociotheological analysis of our culture, we have found the locus of many of these pressures in a spurious secularism that stands over against an authentic secularism and the secular relevance of the church. In the previous chapter we examined the power of organized society more precisely and concluded that the God who is active in this society is calling the church to make responsible use of its own power in service to the world.

Throughout the preceding discussion much of what we

said about the church had reference particularly to the church in its denominational or ecumenical expressions, and in its national posture. We must now turn our attention to the level of the local congregation and inquire what this strategy of Christian action has to do with men and women in their own local congregations and communities; what it means, therefore, for the "equipment of the saints for the work of ministry."

There are over sixty-three million persons in the United States who claim membership in one of two hundred and twenty-seven Protestant denominations. They have joined the church for various reasons. But by far the two most significant facts about the great majority of people who join and remain in the main-line churches are: (1) they are involved in what we call "the life and work of the church" at a very low intensity—mainly by occasional attendance at Sunday morning worship (it is estimated that less than 25 per cent of all church members are active in the sense of regular attendance and participation in one or more church groups); (2) they have no awareness that becoming church members makes them "peculiar people" in the society of which they are a part. This latter fact does not mean that they have a sense of the church's holy secularity which we have already discussed. It simply means—and this is related to the low intensity of their participation—that for them church membership is of no consequence to their total view of reality, the orientation of their values, or their image of themselves as private persons. Indeed, if they believed that joining the church really required "something different" in these respects from that which most Americans share, it is doubtful that they would bother to come at all.

Of course, many people assume that certain observances and beliefs go along with church membership. But the notion is as unconscious as it is widespread that there is an exact correspondence between being and intention, between the person, as such, and the ideals he acknowledges. People who go to church admire the lofty ideals and inspiring goals the minister sets before them, but it is generally quite sufficient to recognize their essential validity. One does not have to live up to them. The minister himself, they are persuaded, does not really intend that they should be actualized *here and now,* in *this* community, by *these* people.

Popularly, church membership means being and doing what all decent, law-abiding Americans are supposed to do. It is segmental—restricted to the narrow province of religion. It exists in an environment that benevolently rewards it with many conveniences and a considerable measure of public esteem. We can say that Christianity in America, whether calculated in terms of active membership in some congregation, marginal membership, or cordial relationship, is a majority religion. As such, church membership pays well and costs little.

All of this means that the great bulk of the people in the pews do not really believe in "the church." They believe in religion. They believe in the voluntary, inchoate fellowship of worshipers whose lives should, all other things being equal, set an example of the best that America offers. But they do not believe in the church as the bearer of a radically new orientation toward the world, as a revolutionary power that penetrates the world in order to help it become attentive to its own purposes. They do not see themselves as the special people of God who have a secular task to perform for his whole people.

This is not to say that the majority of the laity are not loyal churchmen. They love and respect the church they understand, and what they understand about the church is due, to no small degree, to the halfhearted, truncated doctrine of the church they have received from the clergy and from the cultural image. Nor does this criticism presuppose that the local congregations would do well without these people who are peripheral both in participation and in understanding. If the church, to maintain contact with the real world, requires a "hard core," it needs also this "soft periphery."

God has something significant for everyone to do as long as they do not completely frustrate his primary business. It is, therefore, not our purpose to dismiss from the church these "marginal members" whom God himself has not dismissed. All we wish to say is that there is a danger here. These people are the "friendly enemies" of the mission of the church as we have described it. They are dangerous in the sense that their ignorance of the meaning of the church weakens everything it does in the world, that even when this ignorance is dispelled by "Christian education," they will not tolerate a church that gives up spiritual things to mix itself up in the business of the world. They will not break through the walls of their socioeconomic ghettos and chummy coteries to contact and enter into dialogue with the unconventional or alienated people of the community.

Nevertheless, the marginal members are also the church. They are indispensable to the mission in the sense that, for all their often reactionary attitudes and peripheral involvement, they continue to be the main pool from which the lay apostolate is recruited. Moreover, in so far as they continue to identify with the institutional church and present to the powers that be, the image of a "church public," they are important for the social mission. This is, perhaps, not enough to say for people who are loved by God and members of his household, but it is something. Their role in the American churches today is extremely ambiguous. For that reason it is not inappropriate to call them the "friendly enemies" of the church in its secular posture.

Periodically the church has attempted to prune off its dead branches or to create a "church within the church."

Monasticism was such a movement in the third century, growing rapidly after the time of Constantine when the church experienced a great influx of heathen members in all parts of the Empire. In the Middle Ages, sects like the Cathari and the Waldenses in southern France, and the Humiliati in Italy were movements of laymen who wanted to create inner circles of holiness and were bitterly rejected by the ecclesiatics.

The Reformation itself, especially among radical groups of Anabaptists, shared some of this yearning for purity and the desire to separate from the masses who were, from their point of view, only Christian by name. Seventeenth-century Congregationalism, the Wesleyan revival in 1737, and the subsequent "Awakenings" among American Protestants were occasions for various movements to deplore the low estate of religion and call for a renewed practice of the Christian life.

The time may be ripe for a movement within the church today, not in the direction of past reforms and revivals that proposed to make the church less secular, but a movement of those ministers and laymen who would have the church become radically secular in terms of its mission to the world. Today there are murmurings of reformation in the new communicants class approaches, new strategies in the city for opening conversations with secularists who frequent inner-city taverns and coffeehouses, renewal groups like Parishfield in Michigan and the Faith and Life Community at Austin, Texas, and lay academies and vocational groups. Most of these experiments are partly in reaction to the absence of true secularity in the middle-class congregations that have become appendages of the world but have no sense of mission in it.

Although Martin Marty, in *The New Shape of American Religion,* insists that his concept of a new Remnant is a goal rather than a group, he calls for the cultivation of a core of leaders who will constitute through their "deeper commitment," a creative minority movement for the renewal of the church. Gibson Winter, in *The Suburban Captivity of the Churches,* speaks with approval of the small groups of laymen who, in reaction against the meaningless activism of the "organization church" have formed retreat centers and fellowships of prayer and study. He sees them as pointing to new direction and meaning for the church in a mass society.

Another contemporary observer of the church takes a slightly more radical view. Peter Berger, in *The Noise of Solemn Assemblies,* is most outspoken in his criticism of the uncommitted masses who have never thought of the church as mission. Berger believes that the most urgent tasks of the church today in its encounter with the world may have to occur in "supraparochial" settings. "The local congregation," he writes, "can then be left to what it has always done and perhaps will always do in the future— liturgy, preaching, the administration of the sacraments, and whatever educational activities seem plausible to those concerned. Essential tasks of the Christian mission in our society can then be undertaken (radically, if need be) outside the local congregation."

But one must assume that these "supraparochial" tasks will be carried on by Christians, by groups of laymen who have rediscovered the meaning of the church in the world despite the fact of having, to some extent, separated themselves from the institutional church in its local, congregational form.

"Core Groups" and Christian Action

It would appear that although no one is prepared seriously to recommend a radical break with the institution which contains those who see the church as a "spiritual filling station" rather than a missionary outpost, even the denominations are interested in renewal through core groups of laymen, working within and outside the life of the congregation. It would, of course, be an exaggeration to call this new interest in "committed laymen" a new monasticism directed toward the world in reaction to the culturally captive congregation. Nor does this have much of the reforming zeal and missionary activity that came out of the religious revivals of the nineteenth century.

It is our position that no meaningful renewal of the church will come in this society until the Church Captive becomes the Church Militant. No effective mission will result unless the small groups of laymen now being gathered are related to the churches of a given community to which they can give skillful leadership in corporate Christian action. By Christian action in this context, we do not refer only to political and social action but to reaching out to submerged and alienated persons and groups. If the fellowships into which these strangers are brought are secularly militant, Christian action, in this sense, becomes a coherence of evangelism and social action. The word is both proclaimed and demonstrated.

Supraparochial groups, lay centers, vocational fellowships in the factory and the office, have an important role to play. To be quite candid, if a group of laymen is repudiated by a congregation that will not permit it to act in the name of the church, such a group would best continue its work outside the local church with, however, denominational recognition and support if at all possible.

Our particular concern here is with what is possible, albeit difficult, in the local congregation, or preferably, in an organized group of congregations across denominational lines and in one community. Extrachurch groups may be necessary, but the churches of the community continue to have a power potential and a responsibility for renewal that should not be passed over lightly in order to avoid the frustration and political maneuvering that is required to give them leadership. One of the most progressive developments in recent years did not take place on a university campus or at a rural retreat center, but in the midst of a busy city. The Presbyterian churches of Kalamazoo, Michigan, formed a corporate ministry for the entire community through an intercongregational diaconate. Experiments of this kind are suited for the urban community. They have an opportunity for maximum freedom in structure and strategy while still maintaining the strong institutional base essential for effective social witness.

Many people in the churches today, who themselves are too involved in their private lives to do any more than they are already doing, are nevertheless seriously asking: "What is the church about? Which way should the church go?" The church is like a huge moving van lumbering down a narrow road. A U turn, even if it were desirable, is not possible without jackknifing. The only way to turn around or to move in a different direction is to take one of the secondary roads to the right or to the left. In either case, those roads must be reconnoitered. Someone must know what problems of maneuvering and what obstacles lie along the way. That task belongs to a small group on motorcycles who will not only have the courage to probe unknown routes but will be bold enough to take over the wheel and steer in a new direction. "The power of God," writes Charles West, "the reconciling work of Christ, operates, not in a church which meets on Sunday morning and perhaps once or twice during the week, not on the edge of the world, but in the middle of daily life and thought. With all the secular sciences and philosophies and with all the secular groups in society it explores the human problems which arise there, which need the Word of God." (*Outside the Camp,* Doubleday & Company, Inc., 1959.) In our situation this must be the task of small groups, perhaps of one core group of laymen who become the agents of the congregation's infiltration of the world.

A Reconnaissance and Intelligence Force

Any congregation that is committed to Christian action in its community needs to have at its center or very close to it, a group of men and women prepared to be—to use military language—the reconnaissance and intelligence force of the main body. This is not a task that everyone in the congregation will be willing or able to do. There are varieties of gifts and ministries. While a "reconnaissance and intelligence group" must welcome all who would join it, it must be conscious of its own integrity and maintain its own disciplined group life and service. Small groups or cells have backfired in the churches in several ways, but there is little evidence that the majority of church members either rush to join them or resent them.

There are three stages by which a congregation develops and employs a central core of laymen for this task—calling, training, and deployment. Let us now describe them in turn.

When we speak of calling we are not referring to the customary methods of "adding members to the church" by appealing to their religiosity. We have underestimated the power of Christ to make his first contact with people through other means. In many cases people who have little concern for the church as a "religious enterprise" will be called to this work of the congregation. More precisely, many of them will not know what religion is about unless it has to do with charity, with loving involvement in the world at the points of injustice and need.

This is not to say that these people should be appealed to on the basis of activistic "do-goodism" rather than the

Word. It is rather that the Word and the church will be interpreted to them as God's will for the freedom of man to live a human life, to fight against the demonic forces of his own nature that seek dominion over social as well as personal life, to order his life by structures of love and justice relevant to the conditions of society.

Calling, therefore, will involve a challenge to many persons who today are estranged from the church to join in the exploration of new frontiers of service in the name of Jesus Christ. It will confront them with the gospel in terms of its revelation of the true condition of modern man in conflict and contradiction. It will present Christ as God's "yes" to man's humanity and His "no" to all the powers of sin and evil both in man himself and arrayed against him. The church is held forth to these people as the militant company of those who are called not out of the world but into it to affirm and bless worldly life and to help to structure it according to justice, freedom, and the loving service of one life to another.

There are undoubtedly people in the pews every Sunday who are hungering for this kind of interpretation of the faith. Some of them will come forward to join such a core group. But there are many other people whom the church—especially in the great urban centers—has not reached, secular men and women who are disillusioned by its spooky irrelevance to the real world.

For one apparent reason or another—temperament, the recollection of early religious experiences, the disinclination of a husband or a wife to participate—many secularists will never come into congregational life. This should not be considered a sign of our failure when we go into the world. As we learned in an earlier chapter, some of these people have a role to play vis-à-vis the church that makes its own contribution to the work of reconciliation. But as the congregation, through its laity, moves into the places formerly "off limits" to pious churchmen, into the institutions and associational groupings of the community, it will encounter and draw in those secularists whom God has called for the renewal of its life and mission. It may well be that in these days it will be primarily through the calling of these "secular churchmen" into a core group of the congregation that renewal and mission will happen in the urban sector of the church.

What kind of training is needed to prepare a core group for the task of reconnaissance and intelligence in the world? The first thing to be said is that the training of this group is not a once-for-all, isolated experience. Various programs of "leadership training" and courses for "schools of the laity" have been devised for periods ranging from two weeks during the summer to meetings held once a week for a year. What is needed is a program of "continuing education" that will be tailored to fit the particular congregation and situation, and will be flexible enough to meet the needs of lay theologians in various stages of development. This may have to be group training, but a great deal will be lost if special attention is not given to each individual and the secular vocation and cultural activities in which he or she is involved.

Secondly, it should be obvious that the actual involvement of the laity in ministry is the primary occasion for learning about the ministry itself. The deliberate movement toward the world is a learning experience. Reconnaissance is unnecessary when knowledge of the terrain and intelligence about the enemy is already in hand. American churchmen have had almost no experience in this kind of witness. The very fact that we do not know precisely what engagement with the world means, that in most situations we have not even identified the enemy, means that laymen must "learn as they go."

Thirdly, a body of facts, general information, and technique must be gathered together from laymen themselves. One of our problems is that we have not asked the laity to make available for the mission of the church what it already knows about the world in which it lives, which is so often a world different from the one the parson preaches about. A sociologist who had been invited to address a denominational study conference on community power structure said: "This is the first time the church has asked me to make a contribution out of the knowledge and skills of my own profession. I'm usually called on for money or asked to give a Saturday afternoon to painting the Cub Scout room or repairing furniture in the Ladies Parlor."

A number of good books written by both Protestant and Roman Catholic churchmen are available on the ministry of the laity in the world. But no amount of printed resources, filmstrips, and lectures will ever be a substitute for the strategic information laymen possess, often unconsciously, about the real world. Not all laymen, of course, are aware of what is going on around them. Frequently they express astonishment that secular information is relevant to the purposes of the church. Even the simple matter of a man's occupation seems to have no relationship to their image of churchmanship.

A denominational executive reports that at a social action conference of California laymen, persons were deliberately asked to introduce themselves by mentioning their vocations and secular involvements. Introductions, however, proceeded around the circle in the characteristic fashion:

"Bill Smith. I'm a deacon in the —— Church."

"Tom Jones, —— Church. I teach the senior highs and supervise the daily vacation Bible school."

And so it went from one person to another with an almost studied avoidance of occupational and secular interests. Said one layman afterward: "I guess we didn't know what you were getting at. What interest could our jobs and community connections have at a church conference?" This fellow was a local district attorney, a board member of several important agencies, and a delegate to the Republican National Convention in 1956!

But once laymen understand what the church is about and the intelligence it needs for mission they will share important information and educate one another. Knowledge about individual community leaders, the history and development of a town, the way decisions are made in its institutions and social groups, the deals being made in the world of politics and business, the norms and values in the arts and sciences, the presuppositions and operational concepts of the professions—this is grist for the mill of a core group which has the responsibility of planning strategy for the mission of a particular church in an American community. Laymen have this knowledge. In one sense, training has to do with encouraging them to recall it, share it, and analyze it theologically.

Undergirding this kind of practical information and savvy there is undoubtedly a place for a more formal and systematic study program. Certain basic subject matter comes to mind from the successful experience of several lay study centers and congregational academies in this country and abroad. Basic theology for the laity, the nature and mission of the church in an urban society, social ethics, ecumenics, and approaches to Christian social action are some of these. Some congregations have also experimented with discussions on current news events, American history, articles in *Christianity and Crisis* and *The Reporter* magazine, and the images of man which are mirrored in contemporary drama, music, painting, and the novel. Here again such a study program is most authentic when some of the laymen who are participating are writers, artists, politicians, or members of other professions particularly related to cultural problems.

Lay training for mission, however, is not an armchair exercise. Theology and social ethics are developed in the field, in the task of reconnaissance, and in the little skirmishes that every good reconnaissance group sooner or later runs into. News should be made, not simply reviewed by the church. The images of man and society are encountered in the persons and institutions the church works with from day to day and not primarily in the pages of *The New Yorker* and *Theatre Arts*. There is a necessary rhythm of formal study and "action research" that together comprise the training program of the core group and may hopefully spill over into the congregation in the form of conferences and forums.

Let us be clear that this is not a matter of gaining more knowledge about everything that has to do with worldly life. *What we already know and what we discover needs to be ordered in accordance with the Christian understanding of the nature and destiny of man and society.* It needs to be organized and shared in such a way as to assist in the task of what may be called a sociotheological analysis of the world. It must be directed to the specific objectives of a given church in a given community and not canned in a denominational manual or disseminated haphazardly as general information of religious interest.

Finally, we must speak of deployment. Because it is the stage in which action really begins it is our main interest here and the one with which we must conclude the argument of this book.

Deployment refers to a strategy of Christian action implied by what Hans Ruedi Weber and others have called "the scattered church." Most of us assume, as we are reminded by the report of the Evanston Assembly of the World Council of Churches, that the church is already deployed in the world in the form of its laity who are in the factories, on the farms, in the places of business, the schools and homes, of the community. In as much as witness is made to Christ by these laymen, the church is strategically engaged with the world; and what Ted Wickham, formerly an industrial evangelist in Sheffield, England, calls "the secular relevance of the gospel" is openly demonstrated.

It is certainly true that through the vocational life of the laity the church is already scattered in the world. When we speak of deployment, however, we are implying a more deliberate and delicate approach to the world; one that does not depend primarily on the individual decision of each person to bear witness in his own place, but upon the decision of the core group to maintain, through one or more of its members, an outpost in some sector of the community that is the objective of corporate action. Indeed we may speak of corporate action itself as the strategic deployment of the church in the structures of society.

A few congregations have actually assigned laymen to community organizations that needed help or to which the congregation felt a need to be related. This is, in the narrow sense, what we mean by deployment. It is the strategic infiltration of areas of need and centers of decision-making in the community for the purpose of mission.

A reconnaissance and intelligence group, to recall our military analogy, does not deploy itself for carrying on private surveillance of the enemy or engaging in little individual wars here and there. It operates by an agreed-upon plan of scouting the terrain immediately before the main body and reporting back in order that the combat team might move forward and secure the next objective.

Like all analogies, this one has the disadvantage of raising problems which are not intended. We are not suggesting that the church has a series of "objectives," which by attaining brings it closer and closer to the total occupation of the territory of the secular. This may be the strategy of the Communist Party. It is not the strategy of the church. Such an interest has already been barred from our consideration. What we are saying is that particular objectives of Christian action—whether to desegregate a community swimming pool or to begin Bible study among doctors in the Medical Center—requires some technical information, some "inside" contacts, some deployment of a core group which opens the way for the congregation to achieve its ends.

The field of secular vocations, which has been the primary focus of the scattered-church discussions, is certainly not eliminated by this action-oriented approach. Laymen need to be helped to understand the meaning of work in our society and to plan together about how the gospel can become relevant to themselves and to others on the job. Clerical workers in a large insurance company or truckers in a freight transfer station can be brought together through the work of one or two Christians who want to raise questions about the depersonalization of secretaries or the need for a freight-handlers' union. If these laymen have been encouraged to do this by a core group, and if they share their problems and receive advice in conversation with other members, this too is deployment.

Influencing Decision Makers

The organized groups and decision-making centers of a community have not received enough attention as possible areas for the planned dispersal of the laity. In our great urban communities, rapidly becoming the normal context of American life, the influence of the church in many important collectivities may decide whether the public good or selfish interests will prevail. In some cases, such as in a community planning body, this influence—initiated perhaps by several members of a core group—may well be overt. The church will openly advocate certain measures with regard to zoning or relocation through its representatives. Here it participates along with block clubs, the merchants' association, and other groups.

But it is not necessary that every instance of deployment have as its objective the manipulation of power factors to achieve some policy goal. If only the church's conventional image is changed from a self-centered, indifferent institution to that of a deeply concerned observer of public affairs—by simply being in the places where policy is being hammered out—this alone is warrant for deployment in the structures of the community.

During a bitter dispute between the International Ladies Garment Workers Union and the Jenkins Sportswear Company in the Wilkes-Barre-Scranton area, a Union Theological Seminary student was attached to the Pennsylvania state labor mediator in a summer field work project in preparation for an industrial ministry. He had no pastoral advice to give, no pat solutions to recommend to the disputants. He simply accompanied the labor mediator to the interviews with the principals, to the many meetings and court hearings—a silent but interested observer.

At one of the conferences someone from the management side noticed, for the first time, this quiet young stranger who was unaccountably seated beside the mediator.

"Who is this guy, Cohen?" he asked, drawing the attention of everyone to the student.

"This fellow?" smiled the mediator. "Why this is Mr. Dring, boys. He represents the church."

A labor representative bellowed: "The church! What in the hell is the church doing here?"

But no one seriously objected. In fact both sides were evidently surprised and pleased that "the church" was concerned enough to be present in that situation where hostility and anger distorted the humanity of men. From that moment Dring was "in." He continued to play no part in the negotiations, but he became acquainted with three or four of the leaders and during the summer talked with them about the dispute, their own personal problems, anxieties, and aspirations. Sometime later, Cohen, the labor mediator, discussing the project with the author, said with appreciation, "I never knew that the church could be like this."

This is one kind of witness the church can make that is of no little consequence to its mission because someone learns that it is willing to stand beside men in the most exasperating experiences of daily life. In other places, however, deployment may be for the overt or covert use of power. In the South a few white ministers—but unfortunately, even fewer laymen—have, in a sense, worked "behind the lines" of the segregationists to help undermine their effectiveness. Others have spoken out in conferences with officials or white citizens councils and lost their churches and very nearly their lives.

A core group of Negro ministers in Philadelphia, refusing to permit laymen to join them in order to maintain stringent discipline, organized a quiet campaign to force certain employers to end hiring discrimination. They gathered information securely hidden by personnel directors, negotiated according to plan, and organized an effective boycott against a baking company and several oil companies in the area. In Detroit a similar group was credited by the Detroit *Free Press* with being the principal factor in the defeat of the incumbent mayor in the 1961 city election.

In a farming community employing hundreds of migrants, a core group of laymen, led by a seminary student, was able to secure a strong position in a county health board and force a group of farmers to provide adequate sanitation for their migratory agricultural workers. George Todd, a former minister of the East Harlem Protestant Parish in New York City, organized a group of laymen to fight corrupt bossism in a Democratic precinct organization.

These examples, and there are others, are given to illustrate the variety and complexity of Christian action when it is dealing with power configurations. In many cases a labor union, the local Chamber of Commerce, a realty board, a mayor's commission, the P.T.A., or some community organization may be the key to the solution of some local problem, or the means by which "the secular relevance of the gospel" can be made manifest.

Because of their exposed economic position—except when they are working for conservative causes—laymen have not usually been involved in really rough-going Christian action. But this may be more the fault of their ministers than of the laity. We have not known well how to inspire, train, or deploy laymen for sophisticated and effective social action. Ministers alone cannot carry this responsibility for the church. A core group of courageous laymen, working with the clergy and, most desirably, representing a majority of the churches in a community, needs to be deployed in the right places, learning the facts and pulling the right levers. With quiet resolve, with love even for those they oppose and concern for the human values at stake, such a group can make the difference between a community in which the church is merely a cultural parenthesis and one in which it is a factor to be reckoned with.

With the rapid development of metropolitanism few American communities will escape the concomitant problems of residential segregation, deteriorating public schools, physical and social planning, and a host of other problems that will have to be solved by the people who move most decisively and swiftly. What a church that is organized for action can do has been demonstrated in several metropolitan areas across the country. They are few indeed and their ministers and working laymen are lonely, embattled people who are not a little shocked and embarrassed by the role that has fallen to them while their sister churches quietly succumb or sell out and move to suburbia. They cannot help being just a little frightened by the disparity between what they learned in seminary and from educational materials and what it is necessary to believe and do to bear witness to the faith where they are. These fighting churches, led by a core of trained and committed laymen and a few young ministers trained in the period of neo-orthodox social ethics and the historic decision of the Supreme Court against racial segregation, are forging a style of Christian action that has not been seen since the days of Rauschenbusch and Gladden—and with a deeper awareness of the holy secularity of the church.

Robert Christ, the minister of the Seventh United Presbyterian Church of Chicago, has been one of the urban pastors who, with a small group of laymen, is a notable example of the new Christian action. Rev. Robert Christ and his congregation played a leading role in the founding and development of the Organization for the Southwest Community (OSC) in the southwest corner of Chicago covering fifteen square miles and populated by over 200,000 people, 18,000 of whom are Negroes. This organization, whose community "congress" represents several smaller groups of residents, social agencies, and businessmen, some of whom were originally organized to "keep the Negroes out," is a result of the decision of the citizens of southwest Chicago to stabilize their community on an integrated basis and to determine its life. In 1960 it had a budget of $50,000 and a professional staff of five. Its program committees included Real Estate Practices, Home Loan, Urban Renewal, Safety, Education, Traffic and Transportation, and other aspects of life in a heterogeneous, dynamic urban community.

The role of the Seventh Church, twenty-five other Protestant congregations, and eleven Roman Catholic parishes is set forth in a report Robert Christ made in 1961 to a conference of inner-city pastors. The report reads in part: "Seventh Church's early involvement enabled it to have a formative influence on OCS programs and policies. To affect the nature of community organizations the local church must be represented at the time and place at which basic policy is set, boundaries established, membership determined (attempts were made to exclude Negroes living in the fringe neighborhoods) and staff hired. . . . By the time of the second congress a caucus of Protestant ministers was established . . . the caucus selected a 'Protestant spokesman' and 'floor leader' and functioned effectively enough to assure a concerted, positive Protestant voice."

The OSC had a stormy beginning, with the residential segregation question dividing the membership and charges of "communism" and "fascism" and other bitterly contested issues threatening to blow the organization and the tense community apart. A Methodist minister and vice-president of the organization was forced from his church; the Seventh Church lost membership and finances as a result of the withdrawal of members who could not accept the role it was playing in "politics and racial integration." It is to the credit of the presbytery and the United Presbyterian Board of National Missions that the congregation was supported financially and not abandoned to the disintegrating consequences of losing about 15 per cent of its membership.

But neither was Robert Christ abandoned by the central core of his laymen. He speaks of the important role of the church session and the impossibility of being able to continue the work without "the elders' understanding of urban problems and the church's mission." Commenting upon the deepening of faith that was experienced by the laity, he writes: "Because participation in the OSC has made the church's faith relevant and immediately applicable, involvement in community has resulted in growth in the faith for numerous laymen and ministers. The immediate implications of the gospel have become apparent; under stress the church's faith begins to flourish, confrontation with the cost of discipleship creates discipleship. Churchmen involved have declared, 'Now the church is getting down to business'; 'Do they [the critics] expect Christians to do anything other than be concerned about our community?'

"The existence of an effective community organization supplies a channel for the Christian's concern for the neighbor. Instead of preaching love of the brother and redemption of life, and then stuttering when laymen ask 'How?' the church now has an instrument for the expression of obedience. Conscientious laymen need not feel guilty and hypocritical because they have no effective means of practicing what they profess. Provided with a realistic channel for discipleship, Christians will practice —and grow in their faith."

Robert Christ makes another interesting observation about the new spirit that came to the laymen of Seventh Church despite the fact that it had to pare down its budget, eliminate much of the inbuilding "program" of the conventional Presbyterian church, and curtail such normal activities as Christian education, calling, women's work, and administrative responsibility with church boards.

"Active participation in community life has supplied an instrument for the local church to have an impact on mass society; the church has a tool for positively influencing the attitudes and conduct of the many people with whom it has had no direct contact. The visible signs of the renewal of the congregational and community life gave the church a sense of accomplishment, an awareness that it could and was doing something of significance. The effort, cost, and consequences of full participation in communal life compel the local church to rethink its mission to the city and the world. The demands and the controversies of organizing the southwest community have resulted in men taking the prominent role in this undertaking of the church; relatively few women were involved in the first two years [1959 and 1960] of the OSC."

Certainly no conclusions can yet be written concerning the ultimate significance of the decision of this particular church to move into the vortex of the turbulent and always potentially violent situation caused by the sociological transition of southwest Chicago. But it is clear that the Seventh Church has shown a path which can lead to the renewal of community life and of the church itself. As Robert Christ has said, "Mission does not just happen." It requires a group of people, an intelligence and reconnaissance vanguard that will also provoke a fire fight when it is strategic. It needs laymen who are called by God for the purpose, trained with all the wisdom and sophistication experience can give, and who are willing to take the risks of using the forms of power available to them to do the works of love.

The church has always been afraid of prophets who believe that God has revealed to them the course it should take and want to assume command for its execution. And properly so. There is one leader of the church—one Prophet, Strategist, and Commander—and that is Jesus Christ. It may be too much to assume, however, that the main body of American Protestantism is under his direction today in terms of its mission. Faith in him has not ceased in the church. The word is still preached—occasionally with power to deliver. Men, women, and children continue, by the grace of God, to come into a deeper knowledge of themselves, of the meaning of life, and of his claim upon their own lives. But as for the church in its secular vocation, as for its concern for justice and freedom, as for its witness to the judgment and grace of Christ in the affairs of the world, we may well question such a church exists in most American communities today. And to the extent that it does not exist we may well wonder whether Christ or the gods of false secularism command and direct the church in this sector of its life. If there are prophets among us who know the way back and are ready to lead the church to obedience—let them speak and let us follow them as long as their prophecy is validated by the renewal that the Seventh Church and other fighting churches have experienced.

There is indeed a danger of pride and self-righteousness in developing a group of elite Christians who, by virtue of superior knowledge and commitment, presume to renew the church. Certainly there are not two groups of Christians—those with gifts for discipleship and those without. And yet it may be that whatever the danger of the core-group concept, it must be courted in this generation if the church is not to surrender to the principalities and powers that have declared their absolute autonomy apart from the Lordship of Christ. Inasmuch as American Protestantism is still remarkably democratic in polity and highly resistant to "prophetic" minorities, the danger may not be so great as it was in periods when the church was under ecclesiastical hierarchy that fostered the doctrine of double standards of Christian behavior and conferred privileges upon those who found its favor. At any rate, the notorious divisions with Protestantism and the traditional conservatism of the older churches will serve as a counterbalance and corrective to any ill-conceived seizure of power by a revolutionary minority.

This is only to say that although such a movement as we have described seems to be needed in the church at this juncture of history, God alone must decide upon its right to give leadership and discard it when its pride and error destroy its usefulness for his purposes. The American churches, paradoxically, seem singularly equipped both by history and temperament to provide the instrumentalities for this corrective judgment.

What alternatives to the development of groups of laymen and ministers who are committed to the witness in the world and willing to lead are available today?

It is a rare and not a particularly desirable turn of affairs when whole congregations suddenly change their image of the church and assume a witness of active engagement with the world. This is not likely to happen in any case. In most situations Aunt Mary will continue to think of the church in terms of the ladies who come on Wednesday afternoons to sew for the Red Cross. Mr. Jones will still want to confine his church interests to teaching senior highs. Mrs. Smith will never prefer picketing to prayer meetings, nor dialogic conversations with "those awful Beatniks" to program meetings with her friends in the Missionary Circle.

The familiar institutional patterns will continue with few changes. The nominal membership and marginal faith of the majority will provide the main direction for what is done inside the building. The housekeeping chores will still need doing, and some people will be called precisely to those tasks. They are, it may be supposed, important in their own right as long as the church continues its habitual way of life. Indeed such functions may give the continuity and stability necessary for the institution if it is to provide a base point for the secular ministry.

We have discussed the church in terms of a "hard core" and a "soft periphery." Both are sociologically inevitable if not theologically desirable. In the current discussions of renewal the full implications of the "hard core" have often been bypassed. The difficulty of getting laymen to risk their security in social action and the dangers of creating an aristocratic cell group have seemed too formidable.

But if God is calling some men and women to the stabilizing, integrative functions of the church in society, it may be assumed that he is calling others to a radical new relationship to the world. A relationship characterized by reconnoitering the frontiers of the secular where, both in the name of the church and outside of it, the gospel can be declared in new ways and with a new display of its power to build and transform, to plant and to uproot, to burn and heal.

Questions for Study and Discussion

Chapter I. The Protestant Trap

1. The author assumes that the church understands its nature and mission in terms of preaching, soul-saving, and inculcating moral virtues. Do you agree? Analyze the things that happen in your church, from the baptism of children to distributing clothing to the poor. What do these events and activities and the manner in which they are conducted imply about your church's image of itself and its mission?

2. Should the church expect tension to exist between itself and the American way of life? How should it express this difference between church and culture? What is the "something quite different" that the church has to do and to say to America?

3. Do you agree that most laymen and ministers are bewildered by the failure of the church to have more influence in the culture? If we do in fact know what is happening to the church in terms of its lack of influence, why are we unable to do anything about it?

Chapter II. Spurious Secularism and True Secularity

1. What do you think about the criticism of the separation of the sacred and the secular? Would this destroy the meaning of religion for you? How can they be joined in one's view of reality without destroying the legitimate "otherworldliness" in Christianity or doing violence to the practical requirements of living in the world?

2. What do you understand by the "humanization" of technological culture? What is the difference between this and the "Christianization" of culture? Which is the responsibility of the church?

3. What are the opportunities for the church to express a "holy secularity" in the community where you live? What would this mean for the worship of the church, for Christian education, for evangelism, and for the programs of the various church organizations?

4. The Report of the Lay Committee of the National Council of Churches states that "once people have become Christians, they will evolve a government which can be depended upon to administer the affairs of state wisely and well." Why is this true or untrue? How does it check with your experience?

5. How should the church relate to persons who do not believe in Christ or who do not accept the moral standards of Christianity? How would you compare the dangers of such a relationship to those the author associates with "spurious secularism"?

Chapter III. The Faithful Use of Power

1. What do you believe God is doing in the social and political revolution in Africa, Asia, and Latin America? How is his work related to the gospel and to the propagation of faith in Jesus Christ?

2. Where are the "centers of power" in your community? Are the persons in these power structures members of the church? In what way is their faith relevant or irrelevant to the decisions they make in public affairs?

3. What do you believe about the relationship between love and justice? How does the church express a concern for persons which combines love and justice, or is the church's responsibility limited to love—the state's to justice?

4. In which of these instances would it be legitimate for the church to use organized power and how should such power be employed: in a local election, a bond issue for public education, the control of pornographic literature, seeking fair employment legislation?

5. In the incident mentioned on page 46 what should be the response of the congregation to the elders who refused to help the Negro family find a home in their community? Would you consider this to be solely a matter of individual conscience?

6. On what issues would it be possible to secure "consolidated policy and corporate action" among the churches of your community? Would it be wise to seek such unity? How would one go about achieving it and to what end?

7. What is the role in the church for "ecclesiastical politics" and controversy? Why is controversy necessary or unnecessary in the church and how should it be handled when differences are extreme?

Chapter IV. The Equipment of the Saints

1. What do you think of the author's analysis of why people join the church today? What other reasons would you give? Are these motives cause for alarm about the true meaning and purpose of church membership?

2. How would you evaluate the decision of an action group to withdraw from a congregation and continue its activities outside the church if it has been refused support by the majority? What are the alternatives to withdrawal which would not blunt the effectiveness of the witness?

3. What intelligence about the world in which you work and live do you feel would be valuable for the mission of the church? How could such information be used in evangelism and social action?

4. What do you think about boycotts, sabotage, and public demonstrations as forms of Christian action? Can they ever be justified and under what conditions? Is it sometimes better for the church to compromise its ideals and bow to tyranny?

5. Toward what ends should the church be working in your community? What organizations should the church collaborate with and under what conditions and limitations? To what extent should the church seek to control these groups and what are the alternatives to control?